N

M000317431

Hornbook Series

and

Black Letter Series

of

WEST PUBLISHING COMPANY

P.O. Box 64526

St. Paul, Minnesota 55164–0526

Accounting

FARIS' ACCOUNTING AND LAW IN A NUTSHELL, 377 pages, 1984. Softcover. (Text)

Administrative Law

AMAN AND MAYTON'S HORNBOOK ON ADMINISTRATIVE LAW, Approximately 750 pages, 1992. (Text)

GELLHORN AND LEVIN'S ADMINISTRATIVE LAW AND PROCESS IN A NUTSHELL, Third Edition, 479 pages, 1990. Softcover. (Text)

Admiralty

MARAIST'S ADMIRALTY IN A NUTSHELL, Second Edition, 379 pages, 1988. Softcover. (Text)

SCHOENBAUM'S HORNBOOK ON ADMIRALTY AND MARITIME LAW, Student Edition, 692 pages, 1987 with 1992 pocket part. (Text)

Agency—Partnership

REUSCHLEIN AND GREGORY'S HORNBOOK ON THE LAW OF AGENCY AND PARTNERSHIP, Second Edition, 683 pages, 1990. (Text)

STEFFEN'S AGENCY-PARTNERSHIP IN A NUTSHELL, 364 pages, 1977. Softcover. (Text)

NOLAN–HALEY'S ALTERNATIVE DISPUTE RESOLUTION IN A NUTSHELL, Approximately 300 pages, 1992. Softcover. (Text)

RISKIN'S DISPUTE RESOLUTION FOR LAWYERS VIDEO TAPES, 1992. (Available for purchase by schools and libraries.)

American Indian Law

CANBY'S AMERICAN INDIAN LAW
IN A NUTSHELL, Second Edition,
336 pages, 1988. Softcover.
(Text)

Antitrust—see also Regulated
Industries, Trade Regulation

GELLHORN'S ANTITRUST LAW AND
ECONOMICS IN A NUTSHELL,
Third Edition, 472 pages, 1986.
Softcover. (Text)

HOVENKAMP'S BLACK LETTER ON
ANTITRUST, 323 pages, 1986.
Softcover. (Review)

HOVENKAMP'S HORNBOOK ON EC-
ONOMICS AND FEDERAL ANTI-
TRUST LAW, Student Edition,
414 pages, 1985. (Text)

SULLIVAN'S HORNBOOK OF THE
LAW OF ANTITRUST, 886 pages,
1977. (Text)

Appellate Advocacy—see Trial
and Appellate Advocacy

Art Law

DUBOFF'S ART LAW IN A NUT-
SHELL, 335 pages, 1984. Softcover. (Text)

Banking Law

LOVETT'S BANKING AND FINAN-
CIAL INSTITUTIONS LAW IN A NUT-
SHELL, Third Edition, approxi-
mately 500 pages, 1992.
Softcover. (Text)

Civil Procedure—see also Federal Jurisdiction and Procedure

CLERMONT'S BLACK LETTER ON
CIVIL PROCEDURE, Second Edition, 332 pages, 1988. Softcover. (Review)

FRIEDENTHAL, KANE AND MILL-
ER'S HORNBOOK ON CIVIL PROCE-
DURE, 876 pages, 1985. (Text)

KANE'S CIVIL PROCEDURE IN A
NUTSHELL, Third Edition, 303
pages, 1991. Softcover. (Text)

KOFFLER AND REPPY'S HORNBOOK
ON COMMON LAW PLEADING, 663
pages, 1969. (Text)

SIEGEL'S HORNBOOK ON NEW
YORK PRACTICE, Second Edition,
Student Edition, 1068 pages,
1991. Softcover. (Text) 1992
Supplemental Pamphlet.

Commercial Law

BAILEY AND HAGEDORN'S SE-
CURED TRANSACTIONS IN A NUT-
SHELL, Third Edition, 390 pages,
1988. Softcover. (Text)

HENSON'S HORNBOOK ON SE-
CURED TRANSACTIONS UNDER THE
U.C.C., Second Edition, 504
pages, 1979, with 1979 pocket
part. (Text)

MEYER AND SPEIDEL'S BLACK
LETTER ON SALES AND LEASES OF
GOODS, Approximately 400
pages, October 1992 Pub.

Commercial Law—Continued

Softcover. (Review)

NICKLES' BLACK LETTER ON COMMERCIAL PAPER, 450 pages, 1988. Softcover. (Review)

STOCKTON AND MILLER'S SALES AND LEASES OF GOODS IN A NUTSHELL, Third Edition, approximately 425 pages, 1992. Softcover. (Text)

STONE'S UNIFORM COMMERCIAL CODE IN A NUTSHELL, Third Edition, 580 pages, 1989. Softcover. (Text)

WEBER AND SPEIDEL'S COMMERCIAL PAPER IN A NUTSHELL, Third Edition, 404 pages, 1982. Softcover. (Text)

WHITE AND SUMMERS' HORNBOOK ON THE UNIFORM COMMERCIAL CODE, Third Edition, Student Edition, 1386 pages, 1988. (Text)

Community Property

MENNELL AND BOYKOFF'S COMMUNITY PROPERTY IN A NUTSHELL, Second Edition, 432 pages, 1988. Softcover. (Text)

Comparative Law

FOLSOM, MINAN AND OTTO'S LAW AND POLITICS IN THE PEOPLE'S REPUBLIC OF CHINA IN A NUTSHELL, Approximately 450 pages, 1992. Softcover. (Text)

GLENDON, GORDON AND OSAKWE'S COMPARATIVE LEGAL TRADITIONS IN A NUTSHELL. 402 pages, 1982. Softcover. (Text)

Conflict of Laws

HAY'S BLACK LETTER ON CONFLICT OF LAWS, 330 pages, 1989. Softcover. (Review)

SCOLES AND HAY'S HORNBOOK ON CONFLICT OF LAWS, Student Edition, 1160 pages, 1992. (Text)

SIEGEL'S CONFLICTS IN A NUTSHELL, 470 pages, 1982. Softcover. (Text)

Constitutional Law—Civil Rights

BARRON AND DIENES' BLACK LETTER ON CONSTITUTIONAL LAW, Third Edition, 440 pages, 1991. Softcover. (Review)

BARRON AND DIENES' CONSTITUTIONAL LAW IN A NUTSHELL, Second Edition, 483 pages, 1991. Softcover. (Text)

ENGDAHL'S CONSTITUTIONAL FEDERALISM IN A NUTSHELL, Second Edition, 411 pages, 1987. Softcover. (Text)

MARKS AND COOPER'S STATE CONSTITUTIONAL LAW IN A NUTSHELL, 329 pages, 1988. Softcover. (Text)

NOWAK AND ROTUNDA'S HORNBOOK ON CONSTITUTIONAL LAW, Fourth Edition, 1357 pages,

Constitutional Law—Civil Rights—Continued

1991. (Text)

VIEIRA'S CONSTITUTIONAL CIVIL RIGHTS IN A NUTSHELL, Second Edition, 322 pages, 1990. Softcover. (Text)

WILLIAMS' CONSTITUTIONAL ANALYSIS IN A NUTSHELL, 388 pages, 1979. Softcover. (Text)

Consumer Law—see also Commercial Law

EPSTEIN AND NICKLES' CONSUMER LAW IN A NUTSHELL, Second Edition, 418 pages, 1981. Softcover. (Text)

Contracts

CALAMARI AND PERILLO'S BLACK LETTER ON CONTRACTS, Second Edition, 462 pages, 1990. Softcover. (Review)

CALAMARI AND PERILLO'S HORNBOOK ON CONTRACTS, Third Edition, 1049 pages, 1987. (Text)

CORBIN'S TEXT ON CONTRACTS, One Volume Student Edition, 1224 pages, 1952. (Text)

FRIEDMAN'S CONTRACT REMEDIES IN A NUTSHELL, 323 pages, 1981. Softcover. (Text)

KEYES' GOVERNMENT CONTRACTS IN A NUTSHELL, Second Edition, 557 pages, 1990. Softcover. (Text)

SCHABER AND ROHWER'S CONTRACTS IN A NUTSHELL, Third Edition, 457 pages, 1990. Softcover. (Text)

Copyright—see Patent and Copyright Law

Corporations

HAMILTON'S BLACK LETTER ON CORPORATIONS, Third Edition, approximately 550 pages, 1992. Softcover. (Review)

HAMILTON'S THE LAW OF CORPORATIONS IN A NUTSHELL, Third Edition, 518 pages, 1991. Softcover. (Text)

HENN AND ALEXANDER'S HORNBOOK ON LAWS OF CORPORATIONS, Third Edition, Student Edition, 1371 pages, 1983, with 1986 pocket part. (Text)

Corrections

KRANTZ' THE LAW OF CORRECTIONS AND PRISONERS' RIGHTS IN A NUTSHELL, Third Edition, 407 pages, 1988. Softcover. (Text)

Creditors' Rights

EPSTEIN'S DEBTOR-CREDITOR LAW IN A NUTSHELL, Fourth Edition, 401 pages, 1991. Softcover. (Text)

EPSTEIN, NICKLES AND WHITE'S HORNBOOK ON BANKRUPTCY, Approximately 1000 pages, November, 1992 Pub. (Text)

Creditors' Rights—Continued

NICKLES AND EPSTEIN'S BLACK LETTER ON CREDITORS' RIGHTS AND BANKRUPTCY, 576 pages, 1989. (Review)

Criminal Law and Criminal Procedure—see also Corrections, Juvenile Justice

ISRAEL AND LAFAVE'S CRIMINAL PROCEDURE—CONSTITUTIONAL LIMITATIONS IN A NUTSHELL, Fourth Edition, 461 pages, 1988. Softcover. (Text)

LAFAVE AND ISRAEL'S HORNBOOK ON CRIMINAL PROCEDURE, Second Edition, 1309 pages, 1992. (Text)

LAFAVE AND SCOTT'S HORNBOOK ON CRIMINAL LAW, Second Edition, 918 pages, 1986. (Text)

LOEWY'S CRIMINAL LAW IN A NUTSHELL, Second Edition, 321 pages, 1987. Softcover. (Text)

LOW'S BLACK LETTER ON CRIMINAL LAW, Revised First Edition, 443 pages, 1990. Softcover. (Review)

SUBIN, MIRSKY AND WEINSTEIN'S THE CRIMINAL PROCESS: PROSECUTION AND DEFENSE FUNCTIONS, Approximately 450 pages, October, 1992 Pub. Softcover. Teacher's Manual available.

(Text)

Domestic Relations

CLARK'S HORNBOOK ON DOMESTIC RELATIONS, Second Edition, Student Edition, 1050 pages, 1988. (Text)

KRAUSE'S BLACK LETTER ON FAMILY LAW, 314 pages, 1988. Softcover. (Review)

KRAUSE'S FAMILY LAW IN A NUTSHELL, Second Edition, 444 pages, 1986. Softcover. (Text)

MALLOY'S LAW AND ECONOMICS: A COMPARATIVE APPROACH TO THEORY AND PRACTICE, 166 pages, 1990. Softcover. (Text)

Education Law

ALEXANDER AND ALEXANDER'S THE LAW OF SCHOOLS, STUDENTS AND TEACHERS IN A NUTSHELL, 409 pages, 1984. Softcover. (Text)

Employment Discrimination—see also Gender Discrimination

PLAYER'S FEDERAL LAW OF EMPLOYMENT DISCRIMINATION IN A NUTSHELL, Third Edition, 338 pages, 1992. Softcover. (Text)

PLAYER'S HORNBOOK ON EMPLOYMENT DISCRIMINATION LAW, Student Edition, 708 pages, 1988. (Text)

Energy and Natural Resources Law—see also Oil and Gas

LAITOS AND TOMAIN'S ENERGY AND NATURAL RESOURCES LAW IN A NUTSHELL, 554 pages, 1992. Softcover. (Text)

Environmental Law—see also Energy and Natural Resources Law; Sea, Law of

FINDLEY AND FARBER'S ENVIRONMENTAL LAW IN A NUTSHELL, Third Edition, 355 pages, 1992. Softcover. (Text)

RODGERS' HORNBOOK ON ENVIRONMENTAL LAW, 956 pages, 1977, with 1984 pocket part. (Text)

Equity—see Remedies

Estate Planning—see also Trusts and Estates; Taxation—Estate and Gift

LYNN'S INTRODUCTION TO ESTATE PLANNING IN A NUTSHELL, Fourth Edition, approximately 350 pages, 1992. Softcover. (Text)

Evidence

BROUN AND BLAKEY'S BLACK LETTER ON EVIDENCE, 269 pages, 1984. Softcover. (Review)

GRAHAM'S FEDERAL RULES OF EVIDENCE IN A NUTSHELL, Third Edition, 486 pages, 1992. Soft-cover. (Text)

LILLY'S AN INTRODUCTION TO THE LAW OF EVIDENCE, Second Edition, 585 pages, 1987. (Text)

MCCORMICK'S HORNBOOK ON EVIDENCE, Fourth Edition, Student Edition, approximately 1200 pages, 1992. (Text)

ROTHSTEIN'S EVIDENCE IN A NUTSHELL: STATE AND FEDERAL RULES, Second Edition, 514 pages, 1981. Softcover. (Text)

Federal Jurisdiction and Procedure

CURRIE'S FEDERAL JURISDICTION IN A NUTSHELL, Third Edition, 242 pages, 1990. Softcover. (Text)

REDISH'S BLACK LETTER ON FEDERAL JURISDICTION, Second Edition, 234 pages, 1991. Softcover. (Review)

WRIGHT'S HORNBOOK ON FEDERAL COURTS, Fourth Edition, Student Edition, 870 pages, 1983. (Text)

First Amendment

GARVEY AND SCHAUER'S THE FIRST AMENDMENT: A READER, Approximately 530 pages, 1992. Softcover. (Reader)

Future Interests—see Trusts and Estates

Juvenile Justice—Continued pages, 1984. Softcover. (Text)

Labor and Employment Law—see also Employment Discrimination, Workers' Compensation

LESLIE'S LABOR LAW IN A NUTSHELL, Third Edition, 388 pages, 1992. Softcover. (Text)

NOLAN'S LABOR ARBITRATION LAW AND PRACTICE IN A NUTSHELL, 358 pages, 1979. Softcover. (Text)

Land Finance—**Property Security**—see Real Estate Transactions

Land Use

HAGMAN AND JUERGENSMEYER'S HORNBOOK ON URBAN PLANNING AND LAND DEVELOPMENT CONTROL LAW, Second Edition, Student Edition, 680 pages, 1986. (Text)

WRIGHT AND WRIGHT'S LAND USE IN A NUTSHELL, Second Edition, 356 pages, 1985. Softcover. (Text)

Legal Method and Legal System—see also Legal Research, Legal Writing

KEMPIN'S HISTORICAL INTRODUCTION TO ANGLO-AMERICAN LAW IN A NUTSHELL, Third Edition, 323 pages, 1990. Softcover. (Text)

REYNOLDS' JUDICIAL PROCESS IN A NUTSHELL, Second Edition, 308 pages, 1991. Softcover. (Text)

Legal Research

COHEN AND OLSON'S LEGAL RESEARCH IN A NUTSHELL, Fifth Edition, approximately 500 pages, 1992. Softcover. (Text)

COHEN, BERRING AND OLSON'S HOW TO FIND THE LAW, Ninth Edition, 716 pages, 1989. (Text)

Legal Writing and Drafting

MELLINKOFF'S DICTIONARY OF AMERICAN LEGAL USAGE, Approximately 700 pages, 1992. Softcover. (Text)

SQUIRES AND ROMBAUER'S LEGAL WRITING IN A NUTSHELL, 294 pages, 1982. Softcover. (Text)

Legislation—**see also Legal Writing and Drafting**

DAVIES' LEGISLATIVE LAW AND PROCESS IN A NUTSHELL, Second Edition, 346 pages, 1986. Softcover. (Text)

Local Government

MCCARTHY'S LOCAL GOVERNMENT LAW IN A NUTSHELL, Third Edition, 435 pages, 1990. Softcover. (Text)

REYNOLDS' HORNBOOK ON LOCAL GOVERNMENT LAW, 860 pages,

Products Liability—Continued pages, 1988. Softcover. (Text)

Professional Responsibility

ARONSON AND WECKSTEIN'S PROFESSIONAL RESPONSIBILITY IN A NUTSHELL, Second Edition, 514 pages, 1991. Softcover. (Text)

LESNICK'S BEING A LAWYER: INDIVIDUAL CHOICE AND RESPONSIBILITY IN THE PRACTICE OF LAW, Approximately 400 pages, 1992. Softcover. (Coursebook)

ROTUNDA'S BLACK LETTER ON PROFESSIONAL RESPONSIBILITY, Third Edition, 492 pages, 1992. Softcover. (Review)

WOLFRAM'S HORNBOOK ON MODERN LEGAL ETHICS, Student Edition, 1120 pages, 1986. (Text)

WYDICK AND PERSCHBACHER'S CALIFORNIA LEGAL ETHICS, Approximately 430 pages, 1992. Softcover. (Coursebook)

Property—see also Real Estate Transactions, Land Use, Trusts and Estates

BERNHARDT'S BLACK LETTER ON PROPERTY, Second Edition, 388 pages, 1991. Softcover. (Review)

BERNHARDT'S REAL PROPERTY IN A NUTSHELL, Second Edition, 448 pages, 1981. Softcover. (Text)

BOYER, HOVENKAMP AND KURTZ' THE LAW OF PROPERTY, AN INTRODUCTORY SURVEY, Fourth Edition, 696 pages, 1991. (Text)

BURKE'S PERSONAL PROPERTY IN A NUTSHELL, 322 pages, 1983. Softcover. (Text)

CUNNINGHAM, STOEBUCK AND WHITMAN'S HORNBOOK ON THE LAW OF PROPERTY, Student Edition, 916 pages, 1984, with 1987 pocket part. (Text)

HILL'S LANDLORD AND TENANT LAW IN A NUTSHELL, Second Edition, 311 pages, 1986. Softcover. (Text)

Real Estate Transactions

BRUCE'S REAL ESTATE FINANCE IN A NUTSHELL, Third Edition, 287 pages, 1991. Softcover. (Text)

NELSON AND WHITMAN'S BLACK LETTER ON LAND TRANSACTIONS AND FINANCE, Second Edition, 466 pages, 1988. Softcover. (Review)

NELSON AND WHITMAN'S HORNBOOK ON REAL ESTATE FINANCE LAW, Second Edition, 941 pages, 1985 with 1989 pocket part. (Text)

Regulated Industries—see also Mass Communication Law, Banking Law

GELLHORN AND PIERCE'S REGULATED INDUSTRIES IN A NUTSHELL, Second Edition, 389 pages, 1987. Softcover. (Text)

Remedies

DOBBS' HORNBOOK ON REMEDIES, Second Edition, December, 1992 Pub. (Text)

DOBBYN'S INJUNCTIONS IN A NUTSHELL, 264 pages, 1974. Softcover. (Text)

FRIEDMAN'S CONTRACT REMEDIES IN A NUTSHELL, 323 pages, 1981. Softcover. (Text)

O'CONNELL'S REMEDIES IN A NUTSHELL, Second Edition, 320 pages, 1985. Softcover. (Text)

Sea, Law of

SOHN AND GUSTAFSON'S THE LAW OF THE SEA IN A NUTSHELL, 264 pages, 1984. Softcover. (Text)

Securities Regulation

HAZEN'S HORNBOOK ON THE LAW OF SECURITIES REGULATION, Second Edition, Student Edition, 1082 pages, 1990. (Text)

RATNER'S SECURITIES REGULATION IN A NUTSHELL, Fourth Edition, approximately 320 pages, 1992. Softcover. (Text)

Sports Law

SCHUBERT, SMITH AND TRENTADUE'S SPORTS LAW, 395 pages, 1986. (Text)

Tax Practice and Procedure

MORGAN'S TAX PROCEDURE AND TAX FRAUD IN A NUTSHELL, 400 pages, 1990. Softcover. (Text)

Taxation—Corporate

SCHWARZ AND LATHROPE'S BLACK LETTER ON CORPORATE AND PARTNERSHIP TAXATION, 537 pages, 1991. Softcover. (Review)

WEIDENBRUCH AND BURKE'S FEDERAL INCOME TAXATION OF CORPORATIONS AND STOCKHOLDERS IN A NUTSHELL, Third Edition, 309 pages, 1989. Softcover. (Text)

Taxation—Estate & Gift—see also Estate Planning, Trusts and Estates

MCNULTY'S FEDERAL ESTATE AND GIFT TAXATION IN A NUTSHELL, Fourth Edition, 496 pages, 1989. Softcover. (Text)

PEAT AND WILLBANKS' FEDERAL ESTATE AND GIFT TAXATION: AN ANALYSIS AND CRITIQUE, 265 pages, 1991. Softcover. (Text)

Taxation—Individual

DODGE'S THE LOGIC OF TAX, 343 pages, 1989. Softcover. (Text)

HUDSON AND LIND'S BLACK LET-

Taxation—Individual—Continued

TER ON FEDERAL INCOME TAXATION, Fourth Edition, approximately 400 pages, 1992. Softcover. (Review)

MCNULTY'S FEDERAL INCOME TAXATION OF INDIVIDUALS IN A NUTSHELL, Fourth Edition, 503 pages, 1988. Softcover. (Text)

POSIN'S HORNBOOK ON FEDERAL INCOME TAXATION, Student Edition, 491 pages, 1983, with 1989 pocket part. (Text)

ROSE AND CHOMMIE'S HORNBOOK ON FEDERAL INCOME TAXATION, Third Edition, 923 pages, 1988, with 1991 pocket part. (Text)

Taxation—International

DOERNBERG'S INTERNATIONAL TAXATION IN A NUTSHELL, 325 pages, 1989. Softcover. (Text)

BISHOP AND BROOKS' FEDERAL PARTNERSHIP TAXATION: A GUIDE TO THE LEADING CASES, STATUTES, AND REGULATIONS, 545 pages, 1990. Softcover. (Text)

BURKE'S FEDERAL INCOME TAXATION OF PARTNERSHIPS IN A NUTSHELL, 356 pages, 1992. Softcover. (Text)

SCHWARZ AND LATHROPE'S BLACK LETTER ON CORPORATE AND PARTNERSHIP TAXATION, 537 pages, 1991. Softcover. (Review)

Taxation—State & Local

GELFAND AND SALSICH'S STATE AND LOCAL TAXATION AND FINANCE IN A NUTSHELL, 309 pages, 1986. Softcover. (Text)

Torts—see also Products Liability

KIONKA'S BLACK LETTER ON TORTS, 339 pages, 1988. Softcover. (Review)

KIONKA'S TORTS IN A NUTSHELL, Second Edition, 449 pages, 1992. Softcover. (Text)

PROSSER AND KEETON'S HORNBOOK ON TORTS, Fifth Edition, Student Edition, 1286 pages, 1984 with 1988 pocket part. (Text)

Trade Regulation—see also Antitrust, Regulated Industries

MCMANIS' UNFAIR TRADE PRACTICES IN A NUTSHELL, Third Edition, approximately 475 pages, December, 1992 Pub. Softcover. (Text)

SCHECHTER'S BLACK LETTER ON UNFAIR TRADE PRACTICES, 272 pages, 1986. Softcover. (Review)

Trial and Appellate Advocacy— see also Civil Procedure

BERGMAN'S TRIAL ADVOCACY IN A NUTSHELL, Second Edition, 354 pages, 1989. Softcover. (Text)

CLARY'S PRIMER ON THE ANALYSIS AND PRESENTATION OF LEGAL ARGUMENT, 106 pages, 1992. Softcover. (Text)

DESSEM'S PRETRIAL LITIGATION IN A NUTSHELL, Approximately 375 pages, 1992. Softcover. (Text)

GOLDBERG'S THE FIRST TRIAL (WHERE DO I SIT? WHAT DO I SAY?) IN A NUTSHELL, 396 pages, 1982. Softcover. (Text)

HEGLAND'S TRIAL AND PRACTICE SKILLS IN A NUTSHELL, 346 pages, 1978. Softcover. (Text)

HORNSTEIN'S APPELLATE ADVOCACY IN A NUTSHELL, 325 pages, 1984. Softcover. (Text)

JEANS' HANDBOOK ON TRIAL ADVOCACY, Student Edition, 473 pages, 1975. Softcover. (Text)

Trusts and Estates

ATKINSON'S HORNBOOK ON WILLS, Second Edition, 975 pages, 1953. (Text)

AVERILL'S UNIFORM PROBATE CODE IN A NUTSHELL, Second Edition, 454 pages, 1987. Softcover. (Text)

BOGERT'S HORNBOOK ON TRUSTS, Sixth Edition, Student Edition, 794 pages, 1987. (Text)

MCGOVERN, KURTZ AND REIN'S HORNBOOK ON WILLS, TRUSTS AND ESTATES–INCLUDING TAXATION AND FUTURE INTERESTS, 996 pages, 1988. (Text)

MENNELL'S WILLS AND TRUSTS IN A NUTSHELL, 392 pages, 1979. Softcover. (Text)

SIMES' HORNBOOK ON FUTURE INTERESTS, Second Edition, 355 pages, 1966. (Text)

TURANO AND RADIGAN'S HORNBOOK ON NEW YORK ESTATE ADMINISTRATION, 676 pages, 1986 with 1992 pocket part. (Text)

WAGGONER'S FUTURE INTERESTS IN A NUTSHELL, 361 pages, 1981. Softcover. (Text)

Water Law—see also Environmental Law

GETCHES' WATER LAW IN A NUTSHELL, Second Edition, 459 pages, 1990. Softcover. (Text)

Wills—see Trusts and Estates

Workers' Compensation

HOOD, HARDY AND LEWIS' WORKERS' COMPENSATION AND EMPLOYEE PROTECTION LAWS IN A NUTSHELL, Second Edition, 361 pages, 1990. Softcover. (Text)

Advisory Board

[XIV]

CALIFORNIA CIVIL PROCEDURE

IN A NUTSHELL

by

WILLIAM R. SLOMANSON

Professor of Law, Western State
University, San Diego Campus

C. KEITH WINGATE

Professor of Law, University of
California, Hastings College of Law

ST. PAUL, MINN.

WEST PUBLISHING CO.
1992

For

Mary Jayne & Aaron

- W.R.S.

Brenda, Marvin, Terry & Oliver

- C.K.W.

PREFACE

We were not content with preparing the first casebook on this subject. D. Levine, W. Slomanson and K. Wingate, *Cases and Materials on California Civil Procedure* (1991). That publication broke new ground. It provided law schools with a convenient opportunity to offer an advanced course which focuses on the state court system, wherein many of their graduates will practice. This supplement now provides an abridged account of one of the most complex procedural systems in the nation. It is also an accessible guide to many of the significant procedural differences, which impact the choice between state and federal courts in California.

We thus followed two closely related mandates throughout: (1) producing a succinct analysis of California civil procedure; and, (2) exposing different solutions to the same practice problems - in a state containing parallel systems of state and federal procedure.

We prepared this state procedure primer to assist (1) law students, who are taking a course in California Civil Procedure; (2) law clerks or practitioners, who have studied only federal procedure in law school; and (3) professors, who are contemplating an upper division course in state procedure. We thank the following for research assistance: Western State University, Hastings College of the Law, and Stephan Dari (WSU '92).

WILLIAM SLOMANSON

C. KEITH WINGATE

San Diego and
San Francisco
August, 1992

OUTLINE

CHAPTER V. DISPOSITION WITHOUT TRIAL

CHAPTER VI. TRIAL

CHAPTER VII. JUDGMENT-RELATED REMEDIES

TABLE OF CASES

TABLE OF CASES

TABLE OF STATUTES

CALIFORNIA

CALIFORNIA CONSTITUTION

WEST'S ANNOTATED CALIFORNIA CIVIL CODE

WEST'S ANNOTATED CALIFORNIA CODE OF CIVIL PROCEDURE

XXI

WEST'S ANNOTATED CALIFORNIA
CODE OF CIVIL PROCEDURE

TABLE OF STATUTES

WEST'S ANNOTATED CALIFORNIA
CODE OF CIVIL PROCEDURE

XXIII

WEST'S ANNOTATED CALIFORNIA CODE OF CIVIL PROCEDURE

WEST'S ANNOTATED CALIFORNIA
CODE OF CIVIL PROCEDURE

WEST'S ANNOTATED CALIFORNIA CODE OF CIVIL PROCEDURE

WEST'S ANNOTATED CALIFORNIA COMMERCIAL CODE

TABLE OF STATUTES

UNITED STATES CODE ANNOTATED

28 U.S.C.A. - Judicial Code

TABLE OF RULES

CALIFORNIA

CALIFORNIA RULES OF COURT

TABLE OF RULES

FEDERAL

FEDERAL RULES OF APPELLATE PROCEDURE

FEDERAL RULES OF CIVIL PROCEDURE

CALIFORNIA CIVIL PROCEDURE

IN A NUTSHELL

FIRST EDITION

*

CHAPTER I

INTRODUCTION

§ 1-1. Civil Procedure in California Law Schools

Civil procedure professors use the federal model in law schools throughout the country. There are several reasons for teaching only federal civil procedure in California. One is the unfulfilled prophesy that the Federal Rules of Civil Procedure (FRCP) would ultimately engulf - and effectively replace state procedural codes. Another reason is that code pleading was deleted from the California Bar Examination and then law school curriculums. During the last generation, that examination has tested the subject of civil procedure, based solely on the FRCP.

One justification for teaching a federally oriented civil procedure course is the enduring soundness of the FRCP. They are used throughout the nation, in federal courts located in all states. Some states have adopted the FRCP, virtually intact, as their own rules of procedure.

The constant legislative and judicial adjustments to the parallel systems of state and federal procedure present a significant pedagogical dilemma. The prevailing federal model for civil procedure provides the basics and prepares the law student for the bar exam. It does not, however, address the two important practice questions which follow.

1

First, what are the tactical considerations which influence the lawyer's choice between state and federal courts?

There are numerous differences between state and federal procedure in California. The quantity and quality of those differences tends to expand, rather than contract. One reason for this gap is that no one has synchronized the numerous changes to these parallel procedural systems. The state's first discovery act in the late 1950's, for example, was fashioned after an aging federal model that rulesmakers overhauled just several years later.

A second question, bypassed by the federal model, is the following: How does one obtain insights into the "real world" of *California* practice while in law school?

One reality is that the majority of local law graduates will practice in California state courts, long before they do so in the federal courts located in California. Thus, they will be constantly using the California Code of Civil Procedure (CCP).

§ 1-2. Nutshell Content

This Nutshell provides a condensed response to the above questions. It is a simplified overview of California civil procedure - a snapshot designed to help students focus on some important facets of state procedure.

This guidebook undertakes several related tasks. It emphasizes California procedure, while acknowledging significant differences in federal practice. It further addresses the "when and where" of applying California procedure in both state and federal contexts. This book occasionally covers the application of federal procedure in California's state courts. It thus highlights different legislative and judicial solutions to the same procedural problems. Readers may thus anticipate or propose the use of innovative procedural solutions, which have worked in one system or the other.

The materials in this book proceed on a timeline, yielding a sense of order to an otherwise amorphous pilgrimage through the thicket of California civil procedure. This will be a journey over a course consisting of the following eight distinct but connected segments:

- proper court;
- pleading;
- discovery;
- non-trial dispositions;
- trial;
- acquiring the object of the suit;
- appeal; and,
- the effect of prior cases.

§ 1-3. California Court System

California's court system is independent from any other judicial system. It is distinct from the federal courts within California, and from the judicial or legislative pronouncements of any other state.

California's three tiered court structure consists of trial courts of first instance, appellate courts for reviewing tria lcourt decisions, and an uppermost court to promote statewide consistency. The jurisdiction of the trial courts is addressed in Chapter Two on subject matter jurisdiction. The jurisdiction of the appellate courts is addressed in Chapter Nine on appellate review.

At the trial level, there are four courts: Superior, Municipal, Justice, and Small Claims. The composition and jurisdiction of those courts is addressed in Chapter Two on subject matter jurisdiction.

Under the 1991 Trial Court Realignment and Efficiency Act, all counties must develop plans to coordinate Superior and Municipal Court services. Each county thus determines how to best implement the legislative goal of eliminating costly duplication in court services at the trial court level. Certain counties have responded by coordinating both administrative *and* judicial services.

At the appellate level, there are two types of court: District Courts of Appeal, and an Appellate Division of the various superior courts to review Small Claims Court decisions. The state is currently divided into six appellate districts (headquartered as follows):

- First District (San Francisco);
- Second District (Los Angeles);
- Third District (Sacramento);
- Fourth District (San Diego);
- Fifth District (Fresno);
- Sixth District (San Jose).

The California Supreme Court occupies the highest tier. Its discretionary jurisdiction distinguishes it from the lower level appellate courts. The latter must hear post-trial appeals. This court, above the intermediate appellate courts, resolves matters of great public importance, including conflicts among the lower state appellate courts. The chart on the next page illustrates the California court system.

§1-4. Relation Between California and Federal Courts

Two court systems simultaneously decide cases in California: the state courts and the federal courts located with in the state. This section of the Nutshell addresses their relationship.

There are federal trial and appellate courts in California. The state is divided into four federal districts (headquartered as follows):

- Northern District (San Francisco);
- Central District (Los Angeles);
- Eastern District (Fresno);
- Southern District (San Diego).

The decisions of these trial-level courts may be appealed to the Ninth Circuit Court of Appeals (San Francisco). The United States Supreme Court exercises its certiorari jurisdiction to review Ninth Circuit decisions, and certain California Supreme Court decisions.

The relationship between California's state and federal courts is not hierarchical. The state courts are not inferior. The federal courts cannot dictate the result in matters which fall within state competence. Stare decisis does not, for

California Courts

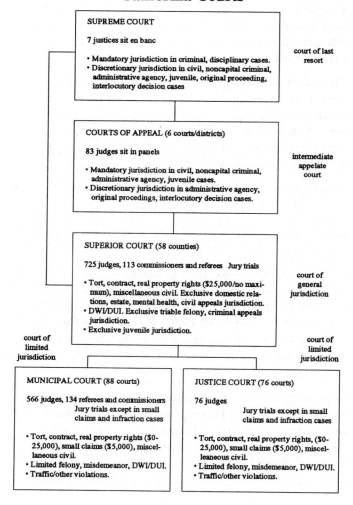

SUPREME COURT

7 justices sit en banc

· Mandatory jurisdiction in criminal, disciplinary cases.
· Discretionary jurisdiction in civil, noncapital criminal,
  administrative agency, juvenile, original proceeding,
  interlocutory decision cases

court of last
resort

COURTS OF APPEAL (6 courts/districts)

83 judges sit in panels

· Mandatory jurisdiction in civil, noncapital criminal,
  administrative agency, juvenile cases.
· Discretionary jurisdiction in administrative agency,
  original procedings, interlocutory decision cases.

intermediate
appelate
court

SUPERIOR COURT (58 counties)

725 judges, 113 commissioners and referees   Jury trials

· Tort, contract, real property rights ($25,000/no maxi-
  mum), miscellaneous civil. Exclusive domestic relations, estate, mental health, civil appeals jurisdiction.
· DWI/DUI. Exclusive triable felony, criminal appeals
  jurisdiction.
· Exclusive juvenile jurisdiction.

court of
general
jurisdiction

court of
limited
jurisdiction

court of
limited
jurisdiction

MUNICIPAL COURT (88 courts)

566 judges, 134 referees and commissioners
        Jury trials except in small
        claims and infraction cases

· Tort, contract, real property rights ($0-
  25,000), small claims ($5,000), miscel-
  laneous civil.
· Limited felony, misdemeanor, DWI/DUI.
· Traffic/other violations.

JUSTICE COURT (76 courts)

76 judges
          Jury trials except in small
          claims and infraction cases

· Tort, contract, real property rights, ($0-
  25,000), small claims ($5,000), miscel-
  leaneous civil.
· Limited felony, misdemeanor, DWI/DUI.
· Traffic/other violations.

Adapted from: D. Meador, *American Courts*, at 86 (St. Paul: West, 1991) example, require the San Francisco County Superior Court to apply any decision of the federal trial or appellate courts located in San Francisco. These are *parallel* court systems, which simultaneously adjudicate matters within their respective domains.

The federal courts operate as an independent judicial system, pursuant to the authority vested in them by the federal Constitution and implementing congressional legislation. Article III § 2 of the Constitution empowers the federal courts to decide matters arising under both federal and state law (i.e., federal questions and diversity).

Federal decisions occasionally affect the relationship between both systems. If the U.S. Supreme Court decides, for example, that a particular subject is pre-empted (controlled exclusively) by federal law, California state courts must then defer to federal law under the federal Constitution's Article VI § 2 Supremacy Clause. If, on the other hand, a federal trial court is exercising diversity jurisdiction in California, its rulings do not necessarily control in subsequent California state court proceedings. They may be binding, however, under the preclusion principles discussed in Chapter Eight of this Nutshell on the effect of prior proceedings.

The "diversity" aspect of federal jurisdiction poses numerous theoretical and practical problems. For example, which procedural law governs when a state case is removed to federal court? The analysis of such problems constitutes the core of first-year *Erie* cases, and upper-division law school courses such as Conflict of Laws and Federal Courts.

California's state courts often exercise their *concurrent* subject matter jurisdiction over federal cases. When adjudicating such federal claims (not within the *exclusive* province of the federal courts), a California court is normally free to use the procedural rules of its own state.

Congressional legislation impacts this facet of federalism in two related ways. First, federal statutes typically create substantive claims which are enforceable in state courts (i.e., concurrent jurisdiction). Second, these statutes are typically silent about federal *procedural* expectations. The impact of such procedural voids may vary, depending on the relevant difference between California procedure and the FRCP. Various sections of this book are devoted to identifying those differences.

There are several important limitations on the *state* court freedom to use state law, when adjudicating federal claims. State courts may not refuse to hear a federal claim, the *substance* of which they might characterize as contrary to their state's public policy. State courts may use their local *procedures*, however, but only in a manner which applies equally to both state and federal claims. See Testa v. Katt (1947). Finally, state court reliance on local procedure may not infringe upon federal substantive rights. See Dice v. Akron, Canton & Youngstown R. Co. (1952).

Jehl v. Southern Pac. Co. (1967) illustrates this federal claim/state procedure theme. The California Supreme Court approved the use of additur, to augment the jury's verdict on a Federal Employer's Liability Act claim. The identical additur procedure would have violated the federal Constitution, if applied in the *federal* trial court just several blocks away (in downtown Los Angeles). California's use of additur, to augment the federal remedy, did not infringe on any federal right of the defendant.

§ 1-5. Sources of California Procedural Law

To practice effectively, California lawyers must know where to find answers to their procedural questions. They must ascertain and prioritize the applicable *sources* of California law.

The term *source* has two relevant meanings. In one sense, it is an authoritative statement of the content of the law; or, a particular rule contained within that body of law. There is a second, related connotation: a source may also mean acceptable evidence of the specific content of an allegedly applicable rule. A CCP section, for example, states a general rule. A case interpreting that section may be evidence of its specific content.

There fundamental sources for determining the contentof California procedural law are as follows:

- the state Constitution;
- legislation;
- caselaw;
- statewide Rules of Court;
- local county rules of court;
- local court policies;
- legislative or administrative histories;
- scholarly publications.

CONSTITUTION The *California* Constitution is much longer (and more frequently amended) than its federal counterpart. It contains a comparatively large number of procedural provisions. The state Constitution generally vests the judicial power in various trial courts. For example, it specifically governs the transfer of cases between certain courts, bases for appellate reversals, requirements for the publication of cases, and judicial disqualifications.

California's Constitution is also a source for certain procedural legislation. It directs the California Legislature to divide the state's counties into appellate districts. Thus, the California Government Code determines which counties are contained in each of the six District Court of Appeals established by the Legislature.

CODES Various California codes contain routine procedural requirements. The California Code of Civil Procedure (CCP) is the most fundamental and extensive. CCP § 86, for example, establishes the basic jurisdiction of the Superior and Municipal Court systems, respective amount in controversy requirements, and the allocation of equitable jurisdiction.

CASELAW California caselaw is another primary source of state procedural law. It contains an evolving body of judicial doctrines, significantly affecting the overall content of procedural law. Caselaw thus expands the total sum of procedural law, to meet new situations not clearly answered by statute. These judicial rules fade in importance when subsequently codified.

RULES OF COURT The California Rules of Court (ROC) are a critical adjunct to legislative and caselaw procedural requirements. While federal rules of court are rarely addressed in law school courses based on the FRCP, California's ROC answer many basic questions not covered by the CCP. ROC 982, for example, contains the numerous legal forms - which are required or recommended for use by California courts.

Each ROC is adopted by the California Judicial Council, under its state constitutional authority to "adopt rules for court administration, practice and procedure." The various ROC thus set forth procedural requirements in the:

- Appellate Rules (Title One);
- Pretrial and Trial Rules (Title Two);
- Miscellaneous Rules, (Title Three);
- Special Rules for Trial Courts (Title Four).

The California ROC are normally mandatory in application. A ROC imposing a greater requirement than the state constitution, however, is merely directory. Thus, a stipulation of the parties - which fails to comply with a "mandatory" ROC, but does not violate constitutional requirements - is not necessarily void. See In re Richard S. (1991).

LOCAL RULES *County* rules of court are guides to local practice requirements. CCP § 575.1 empowers the judges of each superior court to promulgate rules for clarifying local expectations and expediting the business of those courts.

These county rules augment the statewide rules and typically contain procedures not found in either the CCP or the

ROC. Such local rules are changed more frequently. They may be a "trap for the unwary" practitioner from another county.

Each county court must make its rules available for inspection and copying, in every location that normally accepts papers for filing. These courts must also file copies of their local rules with the Judicial Council (JC). The JC then distributes each county's local rules (and amendments) to the clerk's office of all Superior Courts. This filing process thus provides statewide access to each county court's local rules, in addition to the commercial publication of local rules.

Local county rules normally cannot conflict with CCP requirements or California caselaw. County rules may permissibly "conflict" with cases and statutes, however, if there is specific legislative authority for the conflict. County Fast Track rules are a good illustration. They are local rules which permit shorter time limitations than those contained in the CCP (see § 5-15 on Fast Track litigation).

LOCAL POLICIES Local *policies* may also vary from court to court *within* a county. Individual or branch courts have the inherent power to control their proceedings. The Government Code provides that every court of record may make rules for its own government, as long as its policies are not inconsistent with the CCP or statewide Rules of Court.

These policies are typically published in various legal newspapers, under bylines such as "Notices to Attorneys." Lawyers are thus given notice of a particular court's expectations. Notice of local policies is sometimes given by telephone, when counsel's secretary calls the court clerk for a hearing date.

HISTORIES Administrative and legislative histories are useful for interpreting the decision makers' intent. These histories typically contain the debates, reports, and research which culminated in passage of the rule in question. These histories are occasionally cited in the legislative analyses and court opinions interpreting novel procedural issues. The reports of the California Law Review Commission, for example, memorialize proposals and the reasons for legislative changes to the CCP.

SCHOLARLY PUBLICATIONS Books and articles are a secondary source for ascertaining the content of California's procedural requirements. This ancillary source is used by practitioners and judges in formulating tactics and finding solutions to their procedural problems. Scholarly publications thus serve two related purposes. They conveniently summarize the law's development, and predict its direction.

CHAPTER II

SELECTING THE PROPER COURT

§ 2-1. Introduction

A lawyer wishing to prosecute a claim in the judicial system must first determine in what court or courts she may file it. To answer this question the lawyer must consider the issues addressed in this chapter of the Nutshell.

First, the court must have *subject matter* jurisdiction over the dispute to hear and determine the claim. The case must be the type over which the selected court has authority. All courts do not have jurisdiction over all types of cases.

Second, the court must have *personal* jurisdiction over the defendant. This means that the court must have the power to adjudicate the dispute involving the particular defendant. Although the court may have subject matter jurisdiction over cases of the type presented, it may not have personal jurisdiction over the defendant involved.

The defendant also must be served with the appropriate documents in the prescribed manner. Additionally, the plaintiff has to bring the action in the proper locale within the court system. Thus, the lawyer must also consider the questions of service of process and venue in selecting the proper court. This chapter of the Nutshell will discuss how the California courts approach these issues and others which affect the selection of the proper court.

§ 2-2. Subject Matter Jurisdiction

Basic civil procedure courses introduce students to the concept of subject matter jurisdiction. Most cases within the subject matter jurisdiction of the federal courts fall within one of two categories. They are based either on federal causes of action, or arise between citizens of different states with the amount in controversy exceeding $50,000. The courts call the first category federal question cases and the latter category diversity cases. If a case is not within one of these categories, a federal court will probably not be able to adjudicate it.

On the other hand, state courts can generally exercise subject matter jurisdiction over both these categories of cases and over other cases as well. Thus, the major subject matter jurisdiction issue in the California courts is which court within the system should hear a case and not whether it can be heard within the system.

Each county in California has a superior court. The superior courts have original jurisdiction over all cases, except those which the state legislature has by statute given to other trial courts. Cal. Const. Art. VI, § 10.

The counties are divided into judicial districts. Depending upon its population, each judicial district either has a municipal court or a justice court. By statute the legislature has given the municipal and justice courts jurisdiction over most civil cases where the demand is $25,000 or less. CCP § 86.

§ 2-3. Amount in Controversy

If the plaintiff's demand is for $25,000, or less, the municipal or justice court has subject matter jurisdiction over the case. Conversely, demands over $25,000 trigger superior court jurisdiction.   However, a demand of more than $25,000 will not lead to superior court jurisdiction in the following situations: (1) it is made in bad faith; (2) it is not supported by the allegations of the pleading, or (3) the plaintiff agrees to waive any recovery over $25,000.

Courts have been hesitant to find that demands have been made in subjective bad faith. However, if the evidence shows that a demand of more than $25,000 is solely motivated by the desire to have the case tried in the superior court, the municipal or justice court has jurisdiction over it.

Also, the demand may be much greater than $25,000, but the allegations of the pleading may establish that such a recovery could not be obtained. For example, assume a plaintiff demands $30,000 in damages for the negligent destruction of a car. She pleads that the value of the car is only $2,000. The municipal or justice court would have jurisdiction over the case despite the demand. The plaintiff's good faith belief that she deserves the higher amount does not matter. Similarly, assume a plaintiff brings an action for conversion. The demand of $30,000 depends upon the total value of the allegedly converted goods. However, the complaint shows that the plaintiff had only a one-third interest in the goods, while the defendant had a two-thirds interest in them. The municipal or justice court would have jurisdiction over the case, not the superior court.

Claims asserted by the defendant may also determine the proper court. When the plaintiff's demand is less than $25,000, he may properly file the case in a municipal or justice court. However, if the defendant responds with a cross-complaint (see Nutshell § 3-6) against the plaintiff which seeks more than that amount, the case will be transferred to superior court. A defendant's cross-complaint may similarly establish a basis for superior court jurisdiction when a plaintiff seeking less than $25,000 has filed it there improperly.

§ 2-4. Transfer from Superior Court

Initially, a superior court looks to the pleadings to determine whether a demand seeking more than $25,000 has been made in bad faith, or is not supported by the allegations of the party asserting it. If so, the court will transfer the case to a municipal or justice court. CCP § 396.

If it retains jurisdiction, a superior court may reconsider the amount in controversy issue later in the proceedings. Such reconsideration is appropriate although there was a good faith demand which was supported by the allegations of the pleadings. In Walker v. Superior Court (1991), the California Supreme Court held that CCP § 396 authorizes a superior court to transfer a case to a municipal or justice court, if the court finds that a judgment of more than $25,000 cannot be obtained. Thus, if the superior court concludes that a verdict of less than $25,000 will necessarily result from a trial of the case, it should transfer the case despite the sufficiency of the pleadings. In making this determination the court can consider information not contained in the pleadings. Such information may include the result of any judicial arbitration (see Nutshell § 5-12), discovery materials, and settlement conference documents.

The *Walker* court held that after the question of jurisdiction is raised, the parties are entitled to an adequate opportunity to respond. The superior court must allow them to present arguments for or against transfer. If the court complies with these procedural requirements and then decides to transfer the case, an appellate court will reverse only if it finds an abuse of discretion. Consequently, if the decision to transfer is reasonable, it will not be reversed upon appeal, even if the appellate court disagrees.

§ 2-5. Aggregation of Claims

A single plaintiff's claims against a single defendant are aggregated (added) to determine whether the $25,000 limit has been met. On the other hand, two or more plaintiffs' claims will generally not be aggregated to determine jurisdiction. The courts will consider such claims together for jurisdictional purposes, only if the plaintiffs have suffered indivisible harm. Thus, if two plaintiffs have undivided interests as tenants in common in the same property, a suit seeking damages for harm to that property represents a merger of their interests. Consequently, the courts would consider the interests together in deciding whether the amount in controversy requirement had been met.

The federal courts also follow these aggregation rules in determining whether the amount in controversy requirement is met in diversity cases. They, however, require that each individual plaintiff meet the amount in controversy requirement independently. The California courts do not. If the claims of two or more plaintiffs arise out of the same transaction or occurrence, a superior court has jurisdiction if one of the plaintiffs' demands is for more than $25,000. See Emery v. Pacific Employers Ins. Co. (1937).

§ 2-6. Personal Jurisdiction

California courts may exercise personal jurisdiction over any defendant if it is not inconsistent with the federal or state constitutions. See CCP § 410.10. The key question is whether the court's exercise of jurisdiction violates the defendant's right to due process of law guaranteed by the fourteenth amendment to the United States Constitution. The United States Supreme Court has held that a defendant's due process rights are not violated if she was served with process in the state which is exercising jurisdiction over her. Burnham v. Superior Court (1990). Consequently, if a defendant has been served with process in California, its courts can exercise jurisdiction over her. Even if a defendant was not served with process in the state, it may not be a violation of due process for the California courts to exercise personal jurisdiction over her. Examples include defendants who consent to personal jurisdiction and those who are domiciled in California at the time of the suit. Moreover, a state court can exercise personal jurisdiction over defendants without violating their due process rights if the defendants have such "minimum contacts" with the state such that its exercise of jurisdiction would not be unfair or unreasonable. International Shoe v. Washington (1945). Consequently, the California courts can exercise jurisdiction over any defendant who meets that test, no matter where he is served with process or is domiciled.

A defendant may challenge a California court's authority to exercise personal jurisdiction by a motion to quash service of summons. See CCP § 418.10. The filing of a motion to quash is a *special appearance*. On the other hand, if a defendant responds in a way which is deemed to show that she is acting as a party to the lawsuit, she has made a *general appearance*. Filing an answer or making discovery requests unrelated to the issue of personal jurisdiction are examples of such conduct. Once a party makes a general appearance, she is no longer permitted to challenge personal jurisdiction.

If the trial court denies the defendant's motion to quash, she must seek immediate appellate review. If she fails to do so, she waives her right to appeal the trial judge's rejection of her challenge to personal jurisdiction. CCP § 418.10. She cannot make such an appeal after a decision on the merits.

The federal courts do not distinguish between special and general appearances. A defendant wishing to challenge personal jurisdiction may either make a motion to dismiss on that ground pursuant to FRCP 12 or raise the issue in the answer.

If the challenge to personal jurisdiction is rejected by the trial court, then a federal defendant cannot seek immediate appellate review as California defendants do. Instead the federal defendant must await a final judgment on the merits by the trial court. She may then raise her objection to personal jurisdiction on appeal, if the court renders judgment against her.

§ 2-7. Service of Process

A plaintiff notifies the defendant of the suit by serving process on him. Process includes a copy of the complaint filed by the plaintiff and a copy of the summons issued by the court. The summons informs the defendant that he must respond to the complaint within a specified period of time. Otherwise, a default judgment will be entered against him.

California law authorizes several different methods of service of process. The most important, and the most common, is *personal service*. Personal service means that a process server physically delivers the summons and the complaint directly to the defendant. Any method of service other than personal service within California is *substituted service*.

If the defendant is an individual, then the plaintiff must first attempt to serve the defendant personally before attempting any other method. However, if the plaintiff attempts such service with reasonable diligence and is unsuccessful, then the plaintiff may serve the defendant by leaving copies of the documents at his home. The process server must leave them with a competent member of the defendant's household. CCP § 415.20(b). Thus, after two or three attempts at personal service on a defendant, the plaintiff may simply leave process at the abode of the defendant. Espindola v. Nunez (1988). This method of service is called *abode service*. The plaintiff may also leave the documents with a person apparently in charge of the defendant's usual place of business or employment. After leaving process at the defendant's abode or place of work, the plaintiff must then mail a copy of the documents to that address. If he does not, the service is not effective.

How does one serve a corporation? If the defendant is a corporation, the plaintiff may personally serve one of several corporate officials. These officials include its president, a vice president, a secretary or assistant secretary, a treasurer or assistant treasurer, or a general manager. Additionally, the plaintiff may serve anyone authorized by the corporation to receive service of process for it. CCP § 416.20.

Another option available to a plaintiff serving a corporate defendant is to leave process at the corporation's office, with the person apparently in charge; after that, he must mail a copy of the documents to that address. Unlike the rule regarding individual defendants, the plaintiff is not required to attempt personal service before using this form of substituted service on a corporation. CCP § 415.20.

Plaintiffs may also serve both individual and corporate defendants by mail. CCP § 415.30. The plaintiff mails a copy of the summons and complaint, two copies of a notice and acknowledgement, and a self-addressed return envelope (postage prepaid) to the defendant. In order for the service to be valid, the defendant must execute the acknowledgement and return it to the plaintiff within 20 days from the date it was mailed. If the defendant does not do so, she will generally be liable for the expenses incurred by the plaintiff in serving or attempting to serve her by another method. The only way the defendant can avoid such liability is to show good cause for her failure to return the acknowledgement.

The federal courts allow service of process by methods similar to those used in California. Of course, personal service is authorized. However, in the federal courts a plaintiff may use abode service on an individual defendant without first attempting personal service. Moreover, the federal plaintiff need not mail copies of the documents to the address later. FRCP 4.

§ 2-8. Immunity from Service

Traditionally, the California courts granted immunity from service of process to nonresident litigants and witnesses who came into the state to participate in judicial proceedings. Provided that they were in the state only for a reasonable time to attend court, they were exempt from service in another suit. These grants of immunity promoted the administration of justice by encouraging participation in judicial proceedings.

However, the California courts have abrogated these immunity rules. They can now subject nonresidents to personal jurisdiction although they remain outside the state. Thus, the nonresidents generally derive no real benefit from a rule which protects them from service when they come into the state.

Nonetheless, in some cases a California court's ability to exercise personal jurisdiction over a nonresident may be based solely on service on her within the state (see Nutshell § 2-6). In such cases the nonresident would derive an important benefit from the traditional immunity rule. Thus, the California courts may resurrect it for nonresidents who are only subject to personal jurisdiction in the state because they were served within its borders. Otherwise, such non-residents may refuse to participate in judicial proceedings in the state because of fear that they will face service in other suits.

§ 2-9. Venue

Assume a California court has subject matter jurisdiction over the cause of action and personal jurisdiction over the defendant. That does not necessarily mean it can adjudicate the dispute. The question remains whether the court is located in a county which California law has designated as an appropriate one for the resolution of the controversy. Venue rules determine the places within the state where a suit may be adjudicated.

Local actions are those which the law deems to have necessarily arisen in only one place, and venue is appropriate in that place. Cases seeking damages for injuries to real property and those seeking to recover some interest in real property are examples of local actions. In such cases venue is proper in the county where the real property is located. CCP § 392. Actions against defendants sued as executors, administrators, guardians, or conservators are also local actions. In these cases venue is proper in the county which has jurisdiction over the estate which the defendant represents. CCP § 395.1.

Transitory actions are those in which the cause of action could have arisen anywhere. All actions which are not local actions are transitory. In the California courts the general rule in transitory cases is that venue is proper in the county of the defendant's residence. CCP § 395. If there is more than one defendant, venue is proper in the county of any defendant's residence.

However, California law authorizes venue in other counties in many situations. For example, in cases for injury to the person, venue is also proper in the county where the injury occurred. CCP §395. In breach of contract cases, the statute also provides for venue in the county where the obligation is to be performed and the county where the contract was entered.

Despite such provisions, the California courts have displayed a strong preference for trial in the county of the defendant's residence. Their treatment of cases which involve multiple venue rules shows that preference.

Mixed action cases are those in which the plaintiff is asserting two or more claims governed by different venue rules, or cases in which two or more defendants are named who are subject to different venue provisions. For example, assume P asserts both an intentional infliction of emotional distress claim and a breach of contract claim against D. The intentional infliction of emotional distress claim is subject to the general venue provision which requires that suit be brought in the county of the defendant's residence. On the other hand, the breach of contract claim is subject to the broader venue provision mentioned above. Consequently, P's suit is a mixed action case.

The *mixed action rule* applied by the California courts allows the defendant in many such cases to change venue to the county of his residence. He may do so if the plaintiff is asserting one transitory claim which the defendant is entitled to have tried there. Thus, in the example metioned above, if P sued in any county other than the county of D's residence, D could transfer the case there. Defendants' right to trial in the county of their residence is an important one. They do not lose it merely because the plaintiff has joined additional claims which he could bring in another county. Thus, even if a transitory claim is joined with one subject to the local action rule, the defendant may change venue to the county of his residence.

Nonetheless, in Brown v. Superior Court (1984), the California Supreme Court recognized an exception to the mixed action rule. The plaintiffs joined transitory claims triable only in the county of a defendant's residence with claims alleged under the California Fair Employment and Housing Act (FEHA). Venue is proper in the county in which the alleged discriminatory practices were committed in cases in which only FEHA claims are asserted. Plaintiffs sued in that county. The defendants obtained a change of venue on the grounds that none of them resided in that county. The court concluded that the defendants had not been entitled to the change of venue. It held that the legislature did not intend for the wide-ranging FEHA venue provisions to be denied, simply because plaintiffs chose to plead alternative theories of recovery. The strong preference for trial in the county of the defendant's residence was outweighed by the FEHA policy of providing the plaintiff with a broad choice of venue.

The applicable venue rule in a federal court may depend upon whether the case is a federal question case or a diversity case. In both federal question and diversity cases, venue is proper in any district where a substantial part of the events giving rise to the claim occurred and in a district where any defendant resides, if all the defendants reside in the same state. 28 U.S.C. § 1391. In cases in which diversity is not the sole basis for federal jurisdiction, venue is also proper in any district in which in any defendant may be found, if there is no district in which venue otherwise would be proper. Venue is also proper in any district in which all the defendants are subject to personal jurisdiction in diversity cases. Thus, federal law has effectively merged personal jurisdiction and venue analysis in these cases.

§ 2-10. Transfer of venue

When the convenience of the witnesses and the ends of justice would be promoted, a California court may transfer a case to a different county. CCP § 397(3). To establish that the convenience of the witnesses would be furthered by such a transfer, the moving party must submit affidavits which contain the following: (1) the names of the such witnesses; (2) the nature of the testimony expected from each, and (3) why the attendance of each would be inconvenient. Additionally, the affidavits must set forth facts which support the conclusion that a change of venue would serve the ends of justice. If any of these requirements are not met, it is an abuse of discretion for a trial court to grant such a transfer motion.

In deciding whether to grant a transfer motion, the California courts generally do not consider the convenience of the parties to the suit or their employees. But if trial in a distant location would endanger the health of a party who is a material witness, a court will likely consider such facts in making its decision. See Simonian v. Simonian (1950).

The federal statute authorizing transfer on similar grounds takes a different approach. It specifically mentions the convenience of the parties as a factor to be considered in deciding the motion. 28 U.S.C. § 1404(a). There is another major difference between the federal and California transfer schemes. A federal court can only transfer an action to a district where the plaintiff could have brought it originally as a matter of right. Hoffman v. Blaski (1960). Thus, the defendant must have been subject to personal jurisdiction there, and venue must have been proper there as well.

§ 2-11. Forum Non Conveniens

Venue and jurisdictional requirements may be satisfied, but another forum may be more appropriate due to its proximity to the witnesses and evidence. Unlike a federal court, a California court cannot transfer a case across state lines. Consequently, the transfer provisions will not solve the problem when the alternative forum is a court of another state or another country. The doctrine of forum non conveniens is applied in such cases. A California court may thus stay or dismiss its proceedings so that a case can be adjudicated in a more suitable forum. CCP § 410.30. The court may stay or dismiss the case in whole or in part, and it may limit or condition its order.

A California court must first ascertain whether the alternate forum is in fact suitable. If the alternate forum proposed by the defendant would not even adjudicate the dispute, then the California court will. Thus, if the defendant is not subject to personal jurisdiction in the alternate forum, he must stipulate that he will submit to personal jurisdiction there. If he does not, the court will not grant the forum non conviens motion. Similarly, if the plaintiff's claim would be barred by the statute of limitations in the alternate forum, the defendant must stipulate not to raise the defense there.

The trial judge must also decide whether the private interests of the litigants or the interests of the public call for a dismissal or stay. The *private interest factors* are primarily those which relate to whether the trial can be conducted in an expeditious and relatively inexpensive manner. They include the location and importance of the physical evidence, the feasibility and cost of transporting it, the availability of compulsory process to compel the attendance of unwilling witnesses, and the cost of transporting willing ones. *Public interest factors* include protecting local courts and jurors from the burden of dealing with disputes which are of little concern to the local community and weighing the competing interests of California and the alternate forum in adjudicating the controversy.

The defendant bears the burden of proof on a forum non conveniens motion. When the plaintiff is a California resident, this will be a heavy burden to overcome. The state has a strong interest in providing a forum for its residents to litigate their grievances. The plaintiff's choice of forum enjoys a presumption of convenience, when that plaintiff is a resident of the jurisdiction. Thus, the California courts refuse to dismiss an action on forum non conveniens grounds if the plaintiff is a California resident in the absence of extraordinary circumstances.

When the plaintiff is not a California resident, the courts do not give her initial choice of forum the same deference. Plaintiff's choice of a California court itself is not a substantial factor arguing against a forum non conveniens dismissal.

Defendant's residence is thus a factor. If the defendant corporation is incorporated in California, for example, and maintains its principal place of business in the state, California is presumptively a convenient forum. Yet, this presumption is not conclusive. If the defendant can show that the alternate forum is a more convenient place for the trial, the court can stay or dismiss the action.

The California courts have shown a traditional reluctance to grant forum non conveniens motions, when plaintiffs from foreign countries brought product liability cases against California manufacturers. Some courts gave too much deference to the foreign plaintiff's choice of forum. Others adopted the notion that if the substantive law applied in the alternate forum was less favorable to the plaintiff, the alternate forum was unsuitable. In Stangvik v. Shiley Incorporated (1991), the California Supreme Court rejected that view. Instead, it adopted the reasoning of the United States Supreme Court in Piper Aircraft Co. v. Reyno (1981). In *Piper* the United States Supreme Court reasoned that if the courts gave great weight to the fact that the law in the forum state was more favorable to the plaintiff, then they would ordinarily deny forum non conveniens motions. Because plaintiffs could be expected to bring suits in forums where the law was favorable to them, the courts would deny such motions despite great inconvenience. Consequently, the courts generally will not give substantial weight to this factor. Only if the remedy provided by the alternate forum is so inadequate as to constitute no remedy at all will the courts give this factor substantial weight.

The decision to grant or deny a forum non conveniens motion thus remains within the trial court's discretion. Appellate courts will therefore accord substantial deference to the trial court's decision.

§ 2-12. Choice/Conflict of Laws

INTRODUCTION The terms "choice of law" and "conflict of laws" are often used interchangeably. Like the Restatement (Second) Conflict of Laws, this Nutshell does not distinguish between these terms. This section hereinafter uses the composite term "COL."

Practice problems in this field of law arise in two general contexts. First, there is the problem of state/federal conflicts. Federal judges exercising diversity jurisdiction must often choose between state and federal *procedural* laws. This choice is emphasized in the so-called *Erie* portion of the first-year course in Civil Procedure. Second, there is the problem of interstate conflicts. Judges often resolve conflicts between the *substantive* laws of two jurisdictions. This section of the Nutshell analyses the latter context, wherein a California state judge must decide whether to apply the law of California - or some other state - to a particular event.

Why do judges have to make such choices? The United States (and the world) is composed of many states having separate and differing systems of law. Legal issues arise in cases having a significant relationship to more than one of these states. The facts thus present a conflict of laws problem, when the laws of two or more jurisdictions may be applied to the same transaction or occurrence. A special body of rules exists to resolve these problems. This is the COL portion of the law of each state. See Restatement (Second) of Conflict of Laws §§ 1 and 2.

GENERAL APPROACHES There are three predominant approaches to COL resolution in the United States. California practitioners should be familiar with them, in order to comprehend the potential effect of a decision to apply the substantive law of another jurisdiction to a California case.

To illustrate the general approaches in this field, consider the case of two Californians driving separate vehicles in Mexico. They collide, while temporarily across the border in Tijuana. Mexican law limits damages to specified amounts. California law has no comparable limitation.

Some states still apply the First Restatement's historical place of wrong approach to COL problems. Thus, the Mexican damage limitation would not be affected by choice of forum - even if the forum's law did not contain a damage limitation. The application of Mexican law by the California forum would thus bar the plaintiff from obtaining more than the statutory limit on damages where the accident occurred.

Most states currently apply a "most significant relationship" test to such COL problems. See Restatement (Second) of Conflict of Laws § 6. This approach shuns the predictable - but sometimes pointless - application of the law of the place of the wrong. Given the domicile of the parties, for example, California would be the place with the most significant relationship to this controversy. Thus, a California tribunal could readily determine that the Mexican damage limitation is inapplicable. This COL approach typically utilizes a weighing process. Courts thereby determine which jurisdiction's contacts are the most significant, for the purpose of deciding what law would govern the damage issue.

California uses a variant form of the "most significant relationship" approach to COL - premised on a governmental interest approach. See Reich v. Purcell (1967). This is the third predominant approach in the field of American COL. How it operates appears below.

SOURCES A number of California code sections contain COL provisions. Section 1105 of the California Commercial Code, for example, provides that:

> when a transaction bears a reasonable relation to this state and also to another state or nation the parties may agree that the law either of this state or of such other state or nation shall govern their rights and duties. Failing such agreement this code applies to transactions bearing an appropriate relation to this state.

The absence of a contractual COL provision, or the presence of a tort COL problem, necessitates a *judicial* determination of what law governs. Most of California's COL analysis is thus contained in the caselaw.

JUDICIAL APPROACH There are two stages in the resolution of a California COL problem not governed by statute.

First, the court or arbitrator determines whether the conflict is "true" or "false." Assume that two Californians, in separate cars, are temporarily in Mexico. They collide near the border in Tijuana, Mexico. Unlike California, Mexican law limits damages. The foreign jurisdiction would have little or no interest in the application of its laws to a dispute between Californians who are in Tijuana for the weekend. This would be a "false" conflict. If the defendant was a Mexican national, however, this may present a "true" conflict. Each place would thus have a legitimate interest in the application of its laws to this tort action.

The second stage in California conflict resolution is the application of the "comparative impairment" inquiry. Under the leading case of Bernhard v. Harrah's Club (1976) [legislatively overruled on other grounds]:

> Once this preliminary [COL] analysis has identified a true conflict of the governmental interests * * * the 'comparative impairment' approach to the resolution of such conflicts seeks to determine which state's interest would be more impaired if its policy were subordinated to the policy of the other state. This analysis proceeds on the principle that true conflicts should be resolved by applying the law of the state whose interest would be the more impaired if its law were not applied. Exponents of this process of analysis emphasize that it is very different from a weighing process. The court does not 'weight' the conflicting governmental interests in the sense of determining which conflicting law manifested the 'better' or the 'worthier' social policy on the specific issue.

California tribunals thus evaluate the respective governmental interests of the states concerned with the underlying occurrence or transaction.

Recall the variation to the above Mexican accident hypothetical, presenting a California plaintiff and a Mexican defendant. If California's unlimited damages law - and its underlying objectives - would be comparatively more impaired by the application of the Mexican limitation on damages, then California law would be applied.

CHAPTER III

PLEADING

§ 3-1. Introduction

Civil procedure courses use the federal system as the pleading model. While there are some references to state pleading concepts, little or no information is provided about California practice and how it differs from the federal model.

This chapter of the Nutshell addresses many of the same general concepts, but focuses on different California resolutions. It also covers vital matters in California practice, which are not featured in the basic procedure course - such as California's special pleading rules, indemnity, state statute of limitations principles, and diligent prosecution requirements.

§ 3-2. Complaint Nomenclature

There are four types of complaint used in the state and federal courts of California. While they serve similar purposes, the nomenclature differs. It makes little sense to undertake any pleading analysis, absent familiarity with the allowable pleadings and their respective purposes.

Assume that A's car is hit by both B's car and C's car in the same accident. The names of the possible complaints that may be filed, and how they are used, are set forth in the following chart. A more detailed explanation follows below:

SITUATION	STATE	FEDERAL
One: A v. B	Complaint	Complaint
Two: B v. A	Cross-Complaint	Counterclaim
Three: B v. C[1]	Cross-Complaint	Third-party Complaint
Four: B v. C[2]	Cross-Complaint	Cross-claim

[1] Assume that A sued only B.

[2] Assume that A sued both B & C.

In Situation *One*, A sues B *only*. A had the option of joining C, but decided to pursue just one of two potential defendants. A is thus seeking relief from B, for A's damages caused by B's negligence. A's filing is thus called a complaint in both state and federal courts.

In Situation *Two*, B has decided to countersue against A, claiming that it was A who caused the accident. While this is called a counterclaim in federal court, it is a cross-complaint in a California court.

In Situation *Three*, A has still opted not to sue both B and C. C may have some responsibility, however, for causing this accident. The original defendant B may thus join C into A's lawsuit, seeking indemnity from C - if B is ultimately found liable to A. B is a third-party complainant and C is a third-party defendant. B's pleading is called a third-party complaint in federal court. It is a cross-complaint in California.

Situation *Four* differs, because A has joined both B and C as co-defendants (unlike Situations *One* through *Three*, where A sued only B). B is again suing C for indemnity. Unlike Situation 3, however, C is already a party to the suit. B may nevertheless attempt to prove C's sole or partial responsibility for A's damages. This is an action for indemnity between existing co-defendants. The federal pleading is called a cross-claim. The California term is cross-complaint.

Thus, in Situations *Two* through *Four*, the state-court pleading is called a *cross-complaint*. Understanding the

above chart will assist in distinguishing these three uses of
the term cross-complaint in California.

§ 3–3. Pleading the Complaint

STATE FACT PLEADING The plaintiff's complaint
must contain a "statement of facts constituting the cause of
action, in ordinary and concise language." CCP § 425.10.
The substantive law determines what facts are necessary to
properly plead a cause of action. The factual elements of a
viable claim are available in the California Jury Instructions
Civil (see Nutshell § 6-12 on Instructions). Amendments to
these instructions are provided in each issue of West's
California Reporter advance sheets. There are many technical distinctions among the various categories of fact
needed to satisfy California's "fact pleading" requirements.
These distinctions are by no means clear. Fact (or "code
pleading") basically means that a legally viable basis for
suing must be discernible from the facts of the complaint.
The complaint must contain sufficient facts to appraise the
defendant of the basis of the suit. The plaintiff must set forth
a prima facie case - which if proven at trial - would entitle
her to a recovery.

How much must be pled to survive a challenge? There are
some legislative and judicial guidelines. California's rule of
liberal construction of the pleadings dates from the 1872
overhaul of the state's procedure code. When construing a
pleading, "its allegations must be liberally construed, with
a view to substantial justice between the parties." CCP § 452.
Thus, any defects that do not affect the substantial rights of
the parties should be disregarded. And, as stated by the

California Supreme Court in Youngman v. Nevada Irrigation District (1969):

> a plaintiff is required only to set forth the essential facts of his case with reasonable precision and with [the] particularity sufficient to acquaint a defendant with the nature, source and extent of his cause of action. If there is any reasonable possibility that the plaintiff can state a good cause of action, it is error to sustain a demurrer without leave to amend.

FEDERAL NOTICE PLEADING As emphasized in the basic civil procedure course, the federal counterpart to "fact" pleading is "notice" pleading. The federal Supreme Court's primary guidance on notice pleading was provided in Conley v. Gibson (1957): "a complaint should not be dismissed for failure to state a claim unless it appears beyond doubt that the plaintiff could prove no set of facts in support of his claim which would entitle him to relief."

A comparison of these state and federal judicial interpretations suggests the conclusion that California's liberal attitude toward pleading requirements approximates the notice pleading standards applicable in California's federal courts. The state and federal standards are not identical, however.

Assume that the plaintiff files a defamation action, without alleging "publication" of the defamation to a third party. The failure to allege the key element of that tort would subject this complaint to a California demurrer, however, for failure to state a cause of action. In federal court, however, such defects are typically overlooked - where it would be unrealistic to claim that the defendant did not understand the gist of the plaintiff's claim

FORM PLEADING   The California Judicial Council periodically drafts form complaints, cross-complaints, and answers. These forms may be used in actions involving personal injury, property damage, wrongful death, unlawful detainer, breach of contract, and fraud. These forms are drafted in nontechnical language. CCP § 425.12. They are available in the office of the Clerk of Court and in West's *California Judicial Council Forms Pamphlet.*

The Legislature introduced form pleadings in 1979, anticipating that such forms would be mandatory after a brief trial period. One rationale was to limit the attorney's ability to draft case-specific pleadings which were often tested on demurrer. Demurrer-proof form pleadings would have limited California's case backlog by reducing this drain on judicial resources. Due to opposition by members of the Bar, however, legislation which would have mandated the use of forms was rescinded. Thus, form pleadings are permitted, but optional.

SUPPLEMENTAL COMPLAINT   A party may move the court for permission to file a supplemental complaint (or answer) "alleging facts material to the case occurring after the former complaint" was filed. CCP § 464. The events so described must have occurred *after* the original filing, and must directly relate to the original cause of action. A supplemental complaint must therefore allege facts consistent with the rights asserted in the original complaint.

Assume that Seller sues Buyer for breaching their installment sales contract. Buyer breached by failing to pay one or more installments, at the time of Seller's initial filing. If Buyer continues to breach, by missing further payments, Seller may file a supplemental complaint. Alleging this new fact, regarding the subsequent breaches, still relates to the original contract action.

The contemporaneous breach of a *different* installment contract (Contract #2) between these same parties, however, could not be alleged in a supplemental complaint for breach of Contract #1. The plaintiff would either file a new and separate complaint, or an amended complaint alleging breach of the distinct Contract #2.

PRAYER FOR RELIEF The prayer of the complaint sets forth the relief sought by the plaintiff. Plaintiffs must specify the nature of the relief sought, such as monetary or injunctive relief. They may therein request any additional relief they can prove at trial. The common law barrier no longer prohibits obtaining more than specifically asked for in the prayer of the complaint. Thus, a prayer for money damages, seeking X dollars, is not an impenetrable ceiling. The jury may award that amount, and more, depending on what is proven at trial (i.e., X+Y dollars).

California has a special rule governing prayers in superior court actions for personal injury and wrongful death. The plaintiff may *not* state the dollar amount of damages sought. CCP § 425.10(b). Thus, plaintiffs typically alleges that they seek an amount "within the jurisdiction of the superior court."

This limitation was imposed to control adverse publicity. As stated by the Court of Appeal in Plotitsa v. Superior Court (1983):

> the legislative purpose of the 1974 amendment * * * was to protect defendants in personal injury and wrongful death actions from adverse publicity resulting from prayers in complaints, particularly malpractice complaints, for greatly inflated damages claims bearing little relation to reasonable expectations of recovery.

How does the defendant obtain notice of what the plaintiff wants? The defendant may ask for an independent statement of the nature and amount of damages. The plaintiff must respond within fifteen calendar days. Even if the defendant does not make this request, the plaintiff must give notice of the amount sought before obtaining a default, and in any event, no later than sixty days prior to trial. CCP § 425.11.

Federal court complaints normally *must* contain the amount sought by the plaintiff. Special damages, for example, must be specifically stated in the complaint. FRCP 9(g). Otherwise, a federal complaint is subject to a motion to dismiss, or a motion for a more definite statement.

§ 3-4. Demurrers

There are two types of demurrer in California: general and special.

GENERAL DEMURRER The typical demurrer tests the prima facie sufficiency of the complaint. The defendant asserts that, even if the plaintiff's complaint contains facts which are all true, there is still no viable cause of action stated under California law.

The grounds for general demurrer include the following: a lack of subject-matter jurisdiction or plaintiff's capacity to sue; the pendency of a similar action between the parties; misjoinder of parties; and, inability to determine whether the alleged contract is written or oral. CCP § 430.10.

SPECIAL DEMURRER   A special demurrer attacks a pleading which lacks certainty; meaning that it is ambiguous or unintelligible.   A common ground for this form of demurrer is the failure to clearly plead which causes of action apply to which defendants.

Assume that the plaintiff has stated a number of perfectly valid prima facie theories or causes of action in the complaint. If there are multiple defendants and multiple claims, each defendant must be able to discern *which* causes the plaintiff intends to pursue against that particular defendant. One or more of these defendants may specially demurrer. The pleading is unclear about the scope of the plaintiff's intentions. The demurring defendant is uncertain about which theories or causes of action she is defending against.

Several rules of thumb are applied to special demurrers. As stated by the Court of Appeal in Gonzalez v. State of California (1977):

> A demurrer for uncertainty will not lie where the ambiguous facts are presumptively within the knowledge of the demurring party. A special demurrer should not be sustained if the allegations are sufficiently clear to appraise the defendant of the issues

that must be met, even if the allegations of the complaint may not be as clear and as detailed as might be desired * * * [or] such allegations refer to immaterial matters.

What happens after a the court rules on a general or special demurrer?

When a demurrer to a *complaint* is overruled, and there is no answer on file, the defendant is given time to answer - as the court deems just. If a demurrer to an *answer* is overruled, the action proceeds as if there had been no demurrer.

When a demurrer to a complaint is sustained, the court usually grants the plaintiff leave to amend the complaint. Courts are normally quite liberal. They allow a plaintiff multiple opportunities to amend the complaint to cure the defect. The court will sustain the demurrer *without* leave to amend, however, after several attempts; or, on the first demurrer where it appears that the plaintiff cannot possibly recover. That ends the case at the trial level. The plaintiff may then appeal, in an attempt to get the appellate court to agree that a cause of action was properly stated.

One distinction between state and federal practice is commonly overlooked. There are no demurrers in federal practice. The comparable motion to attack a *federal* complaint is one to dismiss for failure to state a claim.

§ 3-5. Answers

The Answer is a responsive pleading, commonly employed for several purposes. It is used to either admit or deny the prima facie case contained in the complaint. And,

Answers typically contain new matter which is unaddressed in the plaintiff's pleading.

ADMISSIONS An Answer may, theoretically, admit all allegations of the plaintiff's case. This is unlikely, because the defendant would probably opt to settle. Defendants typically admit the material allegations which they consider uncontestable. Whether the defendant is a corporation, for example, may be a material allegation for purposes of establishing the identity of the defendant. If corporate status is irrelevant to the defense of the case, however, there is no reason to deny it.

Defendants may also make admissions by not properly denying important charging allegations in the Answer. For example, Plaintiff claims that Defendant implicitly admitted all (or parts) of the complaint. The argument may be based on the code provision that "material allegation[s] of the complaint or cross-complaint, not controverted by the answer, shall, for the purposes of the action, be taken as true." CCP § 431.20. Some of the problems with the form of the denial are covered in the following paragraphs.

DENIALS Answers not intended to admit the allegations of the complaint must contain either general or specific denials. CCP § 431.30.

General Denials A general denial controverts *all* allegations of the complaint. It is both simple and dangerous for a defendant to file general denials as a matter of course. The simplicity evolves from the ability to respond to a complaint with what is essentially a one-line Answer intended to controvert all material charging allegations by a general denial. The danger is that this form of denial, although used frequently, is not favored - particularly in an era when the courts are backlogged with too many cases which should not have been filed, or which should have been settled.

Another danger with the general denial is its potential operation as a "negative pregnant." Such denials can be pregnant with an admission which fails to controvert the complaint. Assume, for example, that Plaintiff pleads that Defendant is liable for a breach of contract in the amount of $10,000.00. Defendant generally denies the complaint containing this particular charging allegation. Here, the general denial is pregnant with the admission that some other amount (above or below $10,000.00) is owed; that is, any amount *other* than the specific amount stated in the complaint. Defendant should have further denied that any other amount is owed.

Specific Denials Any denial that is not a general denial is a specific (or "special") denial.

When is a specific denial appropriate? The hypothetical Answer in the preceding example constitutes a special denial - when the defendant adds (to what would otherwise be a general denial) that she is not liable for breach of contract in either the stated amount *or in any other amount.* This specific denial thus avoids the failure to fully controvert the complaint.

A defendant must specifically deny when the plaintiff's complaint is verified. With the exception of municipal and justice courts, a verified complaint must be controverted by a verified answer. Under the California Rules of Court

(CRC), certain complaints, such as those for marital dissolution, must be verified. CRC 1281. A verified answer must specifically deny each material allegation of a properly verified complaint.

Another form of specific denial is one which is based on information and belief. Thus, when a defendant wants to deny, but "has no information or belief upon the subject sufficient to enable him or her to answer an allegation of the complaint," the Answer may properly place the denial on that ground. CCP § 431.30(e).

AFFIRMATIVE DEFENSES An affirmative defense is new matter raised by the defendant. It does not deny the prima facie charging allegations of the complaint. Rather, it seeks to avoid liability - assuming arguendo that the plaintiff's statement of the cause of action is proper.

Examples of such new matter, normally raised at the time the defendant answers, include comparative negligence and the statute of limitations. A plaintiff's negligence claim must contain facts sufficient to state a cause of action based on the usual elements of duty, breach, causation, and damages. Whether the plaintiff was negligent, and whether the statute of limitations ran prior to filing, are not normally elements of the plaintiff's case. The defendant may raise them in defense, however, by including them in the Answer. Assuming arguendo that the stated elements are true, proof of these defensive matters at trial would allow the defendant to avoid liability.

An affirmative defense is not a denial. It raises a new matter, which does not deny the plaintiff's *prima facie* case.

It is, however, typically filed in a separate portion of the Answer - where it is labelled as "Affirmative Defenses." Such matters are *not* placed in issue by a general denial. The statute of limitations, for example, must be raised in the pleadings. Otherwise, the defendant's attempt to offer such evidence at trial constitutes a variance from the Answer.

§ 3-6. Cross-complaints

The term *cross-complaint* is necessarily ambiguous. It incorporates three distinct pleading scenarios. See Nutshell chart, § 3-2.

What is a cross-complaint? A party who has been sued by another (in a complaint or cross-complaint) may file a cross-complaint, alleging one of the following two matters: (a) any cause of action that he or she has against the person who filed the complaint; and, (b) any cause of action he or she has against someone who may be liable, regardless of whether that person is already a party to the suit. CCP § 428.10 thus provides for permissive and compulsory cross-complaints.

PERMISSIVE CROSS-COMPLAINT The original defendant may file "any" cause that he or she has against the plaintiff. The two pleadings - the plaintiff's complaint and the defendant's cross-complaint - do not have to allege related transactions or occurrences.

Assume that the plaintiff sues for breach of contract. The defendant may cross-complain, alleging an unrelated tort. Judicial economy thus allows unrelated matters to be resolved in one suit, rather than requiring separate actions between the same plaintiff and defendant.

A defendant may also assert a cross-complaint against co-parties and third parties, if it arises out of the transaction asserted against that defendant. CCP § 428.10(b). Original defendants often assert cross-complaints for indemnity against other defendants, whom they believe are wholly or partially responsible for the plaintiff's damages. The same judicial economy rationale also permits this form of cross-complaint, to resolve matters related to the original defendant's liability.

COMPULSORY CROSS-COMPLAINT A cross-complaint *must* be filed by a defendant who wishes to assert a related cause of action against the plaintiff. If the defendant fails to do this, the claim is waived. It may not be made in the context of a subsequent lawsuit. CCP § 426.30.

Waiver is illustrated by the following situation. Suit #1: the defendant fails to plead a cross-complaint against the plaintiff, which arises out of the subject-matter alleged in the plaintiff's complaint. Suit #2: the former defendant finally files her claim as the Suit #2 plaintiff. This plaintiff (who was the Suit #1 defendant) should have pled this cause of action in Suit #1. The Suit #2 plaintiff's claim is thus barred because it was waived when Suit #1 went to judgment.

A defendant's cause of action is related to the plaintiff's complaint if it "arises out of the same transaction, occurrence, or series of transactions or occurrences as the cause of action which the plaintiff alleges in his complaint." CCP § 426.10(c). California courts, and the federal Ninth Circuit, use a *logical relationship* test to determine whether a subsequent lawsuit is barred by failure to plead it as a compulsory cross-complaint in an earlier suit.

Another application of the compulsory cross-complaint rule arises in the federal/state context. Where there is concurrent state and federal subject-matter jurisdiction over a cause of action, California law requires compulsory cross-complaints to be filed in the earlier federal action. As stated by the Court of Appeal in Currie Medical Specialties v. Bowen (1982):

the test requires 'not an absolute identity of factual backgrounds for the two claims [filed in separate suits], but only a logical relationship between them.' * * * At the heart of the approach is the question of duplication of time and effort; i.e., are there any factual or legal issues relevant to both claims? * * * The waiver provision of section 426.30 is mandatory, the policy in favor of hearing all related claims in a single action [is] controlling. The [earlier] 1979 federal action was the proper time and place for Currie's claim.

There are exceptions to the compulsory cross-complaint requirement. Based on the above Suit #1/#2 hypothetical, for example, the waiver provision is not applicable:

- when the Suit #2 plaintiff did not file an answer as the Suit #1 defendant (which is contrary to the federal result);

- when the potential but unpled Suit #1 cross-complaint required the presence of parties over whom personal jurisdiction could not be acquired;

- when the unpled (Suit #1) cross-complaint was the subject of another pending action;

• in small claims court actions; and

• in declaratory relief actions.

Waiver may be excused by application to the court. Suppose that the above Suit #2 plaintiff failed to answer Suit #1. Based on mistake or neglect, the Suit #2 plaintiff may thus request reinstatement of the right to assert this claim, which should have been asserted as a Suit #1 cross-complaint against the Suit #1 plaintiff. CCP § 426.30.

§ 3-7. Amendments

Pleadings are routinely amended during four phases in civil litigation. Parties may first amend at the pleading stage to cure defects. Plaintiff's First Amended Complaint (and any subsequent complaint) is the result of a successful challenge by demurrer. During discovery, a party may amend the pleadings to add new theories or parties after uncovering fresh information. At trial, the parties may expressly or impliedly consent to the trial of issues not contained in the pleadings. Finally, pleadings are often amended after judgment, to conform them to those matters actually proven at trial.

PLEADING STAGE Amendments are readily obtained at the pre-trial stages of a lawsuit. A plaintiff may amend once as of right, prior to answer or demurrer. Judges are very liberal about allowing amendments, when permission is required. Technical pleading defects are thus cured, while avoiding the injustice of failing to litigate cases on their merits. As stated by the Court of Appeal in Douglas v. Weiner (1990):

California courts have a policy of great liberality in allowing amendments at any stage of the proceeding so as to dispose of the litigation on the merits. Indeed, 'it is a rare case in which a court will be justified in refusing a party leave to amend his pleading so that he may properly present his case.'

DISCOVERY STAGE Amendments are routinely granted during the course of discovery, if the proposed amendment is based on "the same general set of facts" as contained in the original pleading. A new cause of action may be alleged, if it spawned by the same underlying facts. One limitation is that the amendment cannot be legally prejudicial to the party against whom it is being offered.

The party resisting the amendment often claims prejudice when a new party is added after the running of the statute of limitations (SOL). Judges may permit the addition of new parties. CCP § 473. The amended complaint then relates back, because it is treated as if it was filed at the time of the original complaint. This theory thus resolves the SOL problem.

The typical scenario for the post-SOL addition of a party involves Doe defendants. California has a comparatively short tort SOL of one year. If the complaint is timely filed, plaintiffs then have an additional three years to locate and serve the defendants (see Nutshell § 3-12 on diligent prosecution). When such discovery efforts are successful, the plaintiff attempts to add a named defendant in the place of an original "Doe" defendant. The "new" defendant - served as "Doe 1" - may seek dismissal, claiming that the relation back theory would constitute a prejudice. The court must determine whether to permit the addition of this new party.

As stated by the California Supreme Court in Austin v. Massachusetts Bonding & Insurance (1951), California courts have been very liberal in permitting amendments adding defendants previously named by fictitious names. "Doe" defendants are thus considered parties to the action from its commencement, for purposes of the SOL. Prejudice cannot be claimed, solely on the basis of the SOL.

These amendments are generally more difficult in California's federal courts. Doe defendants are not permitted; and, it has been historically difficult to add new parties via such amendments. Under CCP § 474, Doe defendants are often added, up to three years after the timely filing of the complaint. FRCP 15(c)(3), however, was formerly the sole provision for adding new parties. It (still) requires that the newly named defendant have notice of the action *within* the time provided for commencing the action. See Lindley v. General Electric (1986).

FRCP 15(c)(1), effective in December, 1991, appears to have liberalized this federal limitation on party joinder. A pleading may now relate back when "relation back is permitted by the law that provides the statute of limitations applicable to the action."

TRIAL STAGE Pleadings may be amended during trial. Such amendments occur in two ways: by stipulation, or by implicit agreement.

Suppose that the parties want to try new issues, not contained in the pleadings. One spouse files a complaint for dissolution, and later decides to try the related issues of spousal and child support. This support evidence would constitute a material variance from the pleading, which sought only dissolution. The court may permit the parties to expressly amend the pleadings to try these distinct issues, rather than require a separate trial on the support issues.

The parties may also impliedly consent to the trial of issues not contained in the complaint. The failure to object to evidence of support, or offering counter-evidence on these new issues, would *impliedly* amend the pleadings. The support issues may thus be tried, where there is no objection to the offer of support evidence. This waiver effectively constitutes an amendment. The judgment may thus include matters not contained in the pre-trial pleadings.

POST-TRIAL PHASE In the above dissolution hypothetical, the trial of unpled issues (spousal and child support) is a variance between pleading and proof. Thus, the party offering the support evidence should make a motion to amend the complaint after trial, to reflect what was actually tried. The courts routinely grant such amendments for the purposes of enforcement and res judicata.

§ 3-8. Indemnity

An indemnity cause of action seeks relief from another party who is or may be liable for the harm done to the plaintiff. Indemnity is sought from co-defendants and third-party defendants (see pleading chart, Nutshell § 3-2). The common bases for California indemnity involve contractual and equitable indemnity.

CONTRACTUAL INDEMNITY A defendant may file an indemnity cross-complaint against co-defendants or third-party defendants to avoid some or all liability, should the plaintiff prevail at trial. The indemnitee (one defendant) attempts to prove that some indemnitor (another defendant) must pay the resulting judgment to the plaintiff. Courts typically delay presentation of indemnity claims until the initial trial phase determines that the defendant seeking indemnity is first found liable to the plaintiff

Due to the freedom to engage in contractual relations, parties often include indemnity clauses in contracts which do not clearly indicate the nature of the indemnity agreement. California courts are often called on, to resolve conflicting accounts of what was meant by the contract.

A number of courts have adopted the approach taken in MacDonald & Kruse v. San Jose Steel (1972). The Court of Appeal therein established a three-tiered paradigm for contractual indemnity in California, as illustrated in the following two-page chart. "T" represents one of the three types of indemnity clause.

Type of Indemnity	Representative Contract Language
T^1	Indemnitor "expressly & unequivocally" indemnifies indemnitee (even when indemnitee is negligent)
T^2	Indemnity "regardless of responsibility" by indemnitee
T^3	Indemnity only if liability "arises solely from indemnitor's negligence"

Indemnitee's Permissible Negligence	No Indemnity If
Either active or passive	(Not aplicable to T1)
Only passive	Indemnitee actively negligent
Neither active nor passive	Any indemnitee negligence

A T[1] indemnity agreement provides the greatest protection for the indemnitee - who may be either actively or passively negligent. A T[2] indemnity agreement provides a middle-ground, in terms of protection for the indemnitee - who may be passively negligent, without loosing the right to indemnity. A T[3] agreement vitiates the indemnity safeguard, when the indemnitee is either actively or passively negligent.

Some California courts do not follow this detailed scheme for resolving the nature of the indemnity relationship between the parties. They look to the language of the particular contract, to determine its apparent meaning.

EQUITABLE INDEMNITY   A party may also seek indemnity, in the absence of a contractual relationship. Co-defendants in tort cases often seek indemnity from one another, and from third-party defendants, under principles of equitable indemnity developed by the California courts.

CCP § 428.10(b) provides for the filing of cross-complaints. It does not specify, however, how the courts are to *apply* indemnity. Under the common law, there could be no relief (in the form of indemnity) among negligent tortfeasors who were *in pari delicto*. Equitable indemnity provided some relief from that rule. California judges required that such indemnity be pled on an "all-or-nothing" basis, however. A less culpable defendant had to allege an indemnity claim by shifting the *total* responsibility for damages to a more culpable defendant. The would-be indemnitee alleged his or her own passive negligence, versus the active negligence of the more culpable party.

The California Supreme Court liberalized the common law "all-or-nothing approach" in 1978. It held that "a named defendant is authorized to file a cross complaint against any person, whether already a party to the action or not, from whom the named defendant seeks to obtain total or partial indemnity." American Motorcycle Association v. Superior Court (1978). Concurrent tortfeasors may thus seek *comparative* equitable indemnity, regardless of the relative degree of fault.

§ 3-9. Special Joinder Devices

This section of the Nutshell summarizes common joinder devices invoked at the pleading stage of a civil lawsuit. They are consolidation, interpleader, intervention, and class actions.

CONSOLIDATION Consolidation reduces the amount of trial time needed to resolve related cases. Thus, a court may order the consolidation of pre-trial hearings or trials for separately-filed cases. There must be "common questions of law or fact [that] are pending before the [same] court * * * and it may make such orders concerning proceedings therein as may tend to avoid unnecessary costs or delay." CCP § 1048.

Assume, for example, that there are a large number of cases filed by different plaintiffs against the same defendant. That defendant is allegedly responsible for an oil spill which harmed their beachfront property. While each plaintiff's property damage differs, the court in which these actions are pending may grant the plaintiffs' motion to consolidate for the purposes of pre-trial discovery motions or trial.

Plaintiffs seeking consolidation thus argue that there are many common facts, and a common question of the defendant's liability. Much of the same evidence would be heard, over and over, if each oilspill case was tried separately. Consolidation would save the time and expense of multiple presentations of the same evidence.

The defendant may counter that it would be prejudiced by the impact of consolidation. The jury may consider the defendant more culpable, due to the presence of multiple plaintiffs suing over the same event.

There are two types of consolidation: complete and partial. When two or more cases are completely consolidated, the pleadings are effectively merged. The allegations of the various complaints are joined as if one, and treated like a single complaint. There is a single decision by the trier of fact. There is one verdict governing all of what were separately-filed cases.

In partial consolidation, two or more cases are consolidated for the limited purpose of a special hearing or trial. The various cases are tried at the same time, solely for the purpose of promoting judicial economy. Otherwise, there would be repetitive evidence if each case were tried separately. Each case nevertheless retains its separate identity. Thus, the pleadings, verdicts, and judgments remain separate. One judgment does not affect another

Consolidation is useful for another reason. There are certain situations where public policy prohibits the joinder of related actions. Under CRC 1212, for example, neither party to a dissolution proceeding may *join* a cause of action "other than for the relief provided in these rules or in the Family Law Act." Public policy requires that California dissolutions be conducted on a no-fault basis. Yet some courts permit the parties to *consolidate* related tort or contract actions for trial, when they are not otherwise permitted to be initially joined in a filing under the California Family Law Act. See, e.g., In re Marriage of McNeill (1984).

INTERPLEADER Interpleader allows a stakeholder to avoid multiple liability or litigation. One who is subject to multiple claims, against the res in his or her possession, may file a plaintiff's complaint in interpleader. The fundamental purpose is to deposit the object of the lawsuit into court, so that those who have an interest in it may interplead their conflicting interests among themselves.

Interpleader may also be filed by a defendant in one of two stages in a suit. Prior to filing an Answer, a defendant in a contract or personal property action may apply to the court for an order substituting another in his or her place. Subsequent to the Answer, a defendant may file cross-complaint in interpleader, when he or she claims no interest in the object of the suit. In either event, the defendant seeks a discharge from liability by the court's acceptance of the res.

Must the interpleader disclaim all interest in the res? This is an important question in cases where an insurance carrier wants to deposit policy limits into court - and yet recover that fund if the insured is found not to be liable.

CCP § 386 is unclear. It provides that the party seeking interpleader "has no interest." The statute also provides, however, that the applicant may "deny liability in whole or *in part*" (emphasis supplied).

California's common law approach prohibited interpleader, unless the applicant had no interest whatsoever. Some 1975 amendments to the interpleader statute were designed to bring California in line with federal interpleader - where the applicant may claim an interest. Thus, it may be argued that the ability to deny liability "in part" did away with the former requirement that the applicant claim no interest in the subject of the action. California case law, on the other hand, appears to indicate that the stakeholder cannot claim any interest. See Pacific Loan Management v. Superior Court (1987).

Federal interpleader unmistakably permits the applicant stakeholder to claim an interest in the res.

INTERVENTION One who is not a party may intervene, to protect his or her interest in the subject-matter of the pending action. CCP § 387. The applicant may claim an interest which aligns him with the plaintiff, the defendant, or neither of them.

The petitioner often presents the following elements: she is so situated that disposition of the action will impair her ability to protect her interest, if she is not permitted to intervene. She argues that the existing parties do not already adequately represent her interests. Her interest must be sufficiently direct and immediate. She will gain or lose by direct operation of the judgment.

The interests of both sides in the existing lawsuit may thus be adverse to that of the intervenor. For example, the plaintiff and defendant may each be claiming title or right to possession of a certain tract of land. Thus, neither party would be asserting an interest on behalf of the hopeful intervenor. Intervention will be normally be denied, however, if one of the existing parties adequately represents the interests of the person seeking to intervene - as where the plaintiff is a governmental entity suing a tractowner to remove hazardous chemicals. An adjacent landowner does not have to intervene, because the government action is filed on behalf of all nearby landowners.

Intervention will be granted, as of right, when there is a statutory right to intervene. For example, the California Civil Code permits the Attorney General to intervene in actions seeking relief from a denial of equal protection under the federal Constitution. The California Corporations Code permits any shareholder or creditor to intervene in corporate dissolution proceedings. Anyone claiming a property interest may intervene in an eminent domain proceeding.

CLASS ACTIONS A plaintiff may file a class action which seeks relief on behalf of not only that plaintiff, but also others similarly situated. A self-proclaimed representative thus seeks court certification of her action as a class action. The relief sought will be for the benefit of all members of the class, not just the individual representative.

The objective is to make the presentation of many small claims a viable option, given the otherwise insurmountable economic burden of proceeding individually. Defendants, that would otherwise escape liability due to the small size of the claim, must compensate the class members as a result of a successful suit.

There may also be a defendant's class action. Thus, one may defend on behalf of all members of such a class.

The basic class action elements are contained in CCP § 382. A class action is maintainable when there is a common question affecting all members of the class, and it would be impracticable for all of them to appear as individuals in the same or separate actions. California caselaw adds further requirements. California also requires that a class action be certified as the superior method for handling the claims of the individual members. There must be an ascertainable class, with a well-defined community of interests. Daar v. Yellow Cab Co. (1967).

The class action device is, essentially, a variant form of the permissive joinder of parties rules studied in the basic procedure course.

California's class action rules are patterned after the FRCP 23 class action rule. The California Supreme Court has thus directed the lower courts to follow the federal class action rules, when there is no California procedural rule on point. See City of San Jose v. Superior Court (1974). California courts also rely on federal decisional law for guidance in interpreting that Rule.

§ 3-10. Truth in Pleading

California judges may impose sanctions for tactics which are frivolous or intended to cause delay. This rule thus governs complaints and cross-complaints filed for improper purposes.

Trial courts may require a party, the attorney, or both to pay expenses and attorney's fees incurred "as a result of bad-faith actions or tactics that are frivolous or solely intended to cause unnecessary delay." CCP § 128.5.

Appellate courts have similar powers. They may add damages to costs on appeal when "the appeal was frivolous or taken solely for delay." CCP § 907. Thus, sanctions may be imposed when a party is responsible for delay or frivolous tactics resulting in an appellate record containing "any matter not reasonably material," as well as "any other unreasonable infraction of the rules governing appeals" (CRC 26a).

Unlike the federal *objective* standard under FRCP 11, the California cases vacillate between requiring just subjective bad-faith, just objective unreasonableness, and requiring *both* for the purpose of imposing sanctions. Most California courts have held that objective bad faith is required.

While the appellate decisions vary, judges often apply CCP § 128.5 sanctions to pleadings under a combined objective "frivolous" and subjective "bad-faith" standard. As stated by the Court of Appeal in LLamas v. Diaz (1990):

> Appellate courts which have addressed the require-ments of the statute are not in harmony. Some are content with the imposition of sanctions where an 'action was prosecuted for an improper motive *or* the action undisputedly has no merit.' Others recognize the need to identify both a frivolous action and its institution or continuation in bad faith. Our study of the legislative history * * * convinces us there must

be an assessment of *subjective* bad faith in addition
to finding a particular action or tactic was frivolous.

§ 3-11. Statute of Limitations

The plaintiff must comply with California's applicable
statute of limitations (SOL) contained in CCP § 312-365.
Neither uncertainty in amount, nor difficulty in proving the
extent of damages, toll the limitations period. Unlike the
commonlaw rule, however, the running of the statute is *not*
triggered by the right to recover only nominal damages.
Rather, the infliction of appreciable and actual harm commences the statutory period. Davies v. Krasna (1975).

Failure to comply with the SOL has at least two consequences for the lawyer and the client. First, it subjects
otherwise meritorious claims to dismissal. Second, it may
constitutes grounds for professional discipline.

There are four (statutory) circumstances whereby California plaintiffs can avoid a SOL that would otherwise expire.
First, when an action arising in another state or country is
barred there, it is normally barred in California. It *may* be
maintained, however, if the plaintiff is domiciled in California. Second, the SOL is tolled if the defendant is not in
California when the cause of action arises. It must be
commenced, however, within the statutory period after the
defendant's return to the state. Third, the SOL is tolled when
the plaintiff is incapacitated. Examples include plaintiffs
who are minors, insane, or imprisoned. Fourth, the SOL can
be waived. The person obligated must sign an appropriate
writing.

A California plaintiff tolls the SOL by filing the complaint. In some other states, the plaintiff must also *serve* the complaint on the defendant, in addition to filing the complaint with the court. Federal courts in California use the state rule, so that only filing is necessary to comply with applicable federal SOLs.

Federal courts routinely borrow state SOLs for diversity cases, and for federal claims arising under statutes passed *prior* to December 1, 1990. For federal claims arising under later statutes, there is a four-year SOL - unless the statute specifically provides for another period. The following chart below depicts the applicable SOLs:

SCENARIO	STATUTE OF LIMITATIONS
Federal statute enacted by Congress before and after 12/1/90	Stautory SOL (if given)
Federal statute enacted by Congress before 12/1/90 (silent)	Analogous California SOL
Federal statute enacted by Congress after 12/1/90 (silent)	Four Years
Diversity	California SOL

The term "FS" refers to a federal statute enacted by Congress. The right column contains the applicable SOL. The term "silent" means that the federal statute does not contain a specific SOL.

There are two types of SOL. The difference results in applying a given SOL from the *accrual* date or from the *discovery* date. The usual SOL begins to run on the date of the injury or breach. That is the date when the cause of action "accrues." So-called discovery SOLs provide assistance to certain plaintiffs, who are entitled to a longer period under special circumstances. The existence of a special relationship effectively generates an augmented SOL, when the defendant with a special duty has taken advantage of the plaintiff in their relationship.

Under CCP § 340.6(a), the SOL for attorney malpractice is one year after the plaintiff "discovers, or through the use of reasonable diligence should have discovered, the facts * * * or four years from the date of the wrongful act or omission, whichever occurs first." This augmented form of SOL is also used in cases involving childhood sexual abuse, asbestos exposure, and health care service providers.

What happens when a plaintiff files the complaint in the wrong state or federal court in California? Assume that a case is filed in federal court within the applicable SOL. It subsequently expires. The court decides that it has no subject-matter jurisdiction. A form of "equitable tolling" preserves the plaintiff's ability to refile the case in state court. Equitable considerations permit a subsequent filing to relate back. The second suit in state court is treated as if it had been filed at the time of the first filing in federal court (prior to the running of the SOL).

As stated by the California Supreme Court in Addison v. State of California (1978):

application of the doctrine of equitable tolling requires timely notice, and lack of prejudice, to the
defendant, and reasonable and good faith conduct on
the part of the plaintiff. * * * [T]he federal court,
without prejudice, declined to assert jurisdiction over
a timely filed state law cause of action and plaintiffs
thereafter timely promptly asserted that cause in the
proper state court.

The federal courts also apply equitable tolling when a case
is misfiled in a California court.

§ 3-12. Diligent Prosecution

The purpose of the SOL is distinct from that of California's
diligent prosecution statutes. The SOL is concerned only
with the timeliness of instituting an action. A diligent
prosecution statute is concerned with speedy prosecution of
an action, *after* it is commenced. After tolling the SOL by
filing the complaint, the plaintiff must then diligently prosecute his or her suit - to avoid dismissal for failure to
prosecute.

The responsibility to timely prosecute arises in both
service and post-service contexts. The basic requirements
are set forth in CCP § 583.110 et seq.

SERVICE REQUIREMENTS There are at least two
different timeframes which thus govern prompt service of
the complaint (which has been timely filed). First, defendants must be served within three years of the filing of the
complaint under the CCP. Second, this service period is
greatly reduced for Fast Track cases (see Nutshell § 5-15).
The service period is only sixty days in many of the Califor-

nia county Fast Track programs. Further, this service period
may be different in certain counties, depending on local
county rules.

POST-SERVICE REQUIREMENTS Assume that the
plaintiff's attorney tolls the SOL by a timely filing. She then
timely serves the defendant. She has further diligent prosecution obligations. The court has the discretion to dismiss,
for example, for a lack of activity after two years or for
failure to bring to trial. And, the case *must* be dismissed if
it is not brought to trial within five years from the filing of
the complaint.

EXCEPTIONS The various diligent prosecution requirements may be extended. The most common basis is that
bringing the action to trial was "impossible, impracticable,
or futile" (CCP § 583.340).

FEDERAL PRACTICE The complaint must be served
within four months of the filing of a federal complaint.
FRCP 4(j). This period differs from any of the California
service periods set forth earlier in this section of the Nutshell.

Federal plaintiffs must take reasonable steps to bring their
cases to trial. Under local rules of the federal districts in
California, it is common practice to require the plaintiff to
appear after six months of inactivity, to show cause why the
case should not be dismissed for lack of prosecution.

§ 3-13. Motion Practice

The terms order, motion, and judgment should be distinguished. The judgment is normally made at the conclusion
of a case. Prior to judgment, the court may issue a number

of orders. Orders are written directions to a party to do something, or to refrain from acting in a certain way. A motion is an application for an order from a judge.

Motions are normally made in writing. Some trial motions may be made orally. Prior to trial, however, the parties normally provide written notice of a motion to the court - and the other parties who have appeared in the case.

Under CCP § 1010, a motion consists of three parts:

* notice of the motion;

* memorandum of points and authorities; and

* evidence on which the motion is based.

The notice of the motion states when and where the motion will be heard. A memorandum of points and authorities must accompany the motion. It contains the statement of facts, law, evidence, and argument relied on in support of (or in opposition to) the motion. CRC 301-387 provide the general format and other particulars for motion practice.

There are minimum notice requirements for California motions. Most motions must be filed and served on the other parties fifteen calendar days before the hearing. Opposing papers must be served five calendar days before the hearing; and the moving party's reply papers, no later than two calendar days prior to the hearing. Service by mail adds at least five days to the minimum time required for notice. CCP § 1005(b).

Memorandums, filed in support of motions, are subject to page lengths. They should not exceed twenty pages. Memorandums over fifteen pages must also include an opening summary of argument. Memorandums over ten pages must also contain a table of contents and a table of authorities. CRC 313(d).

Counsel for both parties normally attend the hearing. The moving party, and then the party opposing the motion or orally present the respective arguments. Parties may make telephonic appearances, under CCP § 1006.5 and various local rules.

Proof of service is not an idle act. Why? Failure to file responsive papers, or to appear, provides the court with the discretion to rule against the offending party. This discretion may not be invoked, however, in the absence of proof of service. Such proof establishes whether the moving party properly served the motion papers. Judges are particularly concerned about the availability of such proof, when a motion is - for some reason - unopposed. Thus, proof of service must be filed no later than five calendar days prior to the hearing.

CHAPTER IV

DISCOVERY

§ 4-1. Introduction

California law schools have used a variety of approaches to teaching the discovery phase of civil litigation. Historically, discovery has been (a) treated as a minor segment of the introductory civil procedure course; or (b) assigned, but not covered in class; or (c) not taught at all. Some schools have offered an upper-division elective on discovery.

Modernly, many civil procedure instructors are emphasizing this stage of a civil lawsuit. Why? Few graduates will spend much time on jurisdictional problems. Virtually all, however, will encounter discovery problems throughout their professional careers.

This chapter of the Nutshell overviews civil discovery in California. It incorporates some important differences in federal discovery practice. The reader will see how the same discovery problems generate different solutions in the state and federal courts of California.

§ 4-2. General Discovery Principles

California's discovery regime is based on the federal model. An enduring description of California's initial 1956 Discovery Act examines the symmetry of the respective rules, and illustrates the legislative intent which inaugurated modern California discovery:

> The enactment of present sections 2016-2035 [current §§ 2016-2036], Code of Civil Procedure, was proposed to the legislature as an adoption by this state of federal rules of procedure relative to discovery and with the express purpose of broadening discovery proceedings in California to the end that they would be comparable with those proceedings in federal courts. These statutes are, in substance, exact counterparts of the federal rules. Therefore, the legislature must have intended that they should have the same meaning, force and effect as have been given the federal rules by the federal courts. Crummer v. Beeler (1960).

What are the essential purposes of the discovery stage of a civil lawsuit?

The discovery phase of a civil lawsuit fleshes out the skeletal detail which is grudgingly relinquished at the pleading stage. California is a "code pleading" state, thus requiring more detail than federal "notice pleading" principles (see Nutshell §3-3). The boilerplate allegations of a demurrer-proof complaint, however, do little to acquaint adversaries with the particulars of the underlying claim. Thus, uncovering the additional details necessary for trial is a principle aim of the discovery stage.

Discovery also *narrows* the issues. As the adversaries unveil relevant information, they are better equipped to determine what are - and what are not - the critical issues. Assume, for example, that the defendant discovers information, during a deposition or document examination, demonstrating his or her lack of liability. That case becomes an instant candidate for summary judgment. A successful motion would screen this case from the system before trial.

A related reason for discovery is to promote settlement. Approximately ninety per cent of California's cases settle prior to trial. This percentage is even higher in certain metropolitan counties. Discovery has a major influence on such results. Once the factors affecting settlement value are uncovered, through formal or informal discovery efforts, it is simpler to compute reasonable offers and demands.

These general purposes of discovery are succinctly restated in Greyhound v. Superior Court (1961). This prominent opinion still functions as a beacon for interpreting California's discovery philosophy:

> The new system, as did the federal system, was intended to accomplish the following results: (1) to give greater assistance to the parties in ascertaining the truth and in checking and preventing perjury; (2) to provide an effective means of detecting and exposing false, fraudulent and sham claims and defenses;

(3) to make available, in a simple, convenient and inexpensive way, facts which otherwise could not be proved except with great difficulty; (4) to educate the parties in advance of trial as to the real value of their claims and defenses, thereby encouraging settlements; (5) to expedite litigation; (6) to safeguard against surprise; (7) to prevent delay; (8) to simplify and narrow the issues; and, (9) to expedite and facilitate both preparation and trial.

The following sections of this Chapter examine the general parameters of California discovery, the specific operation of the various discovery devices, and methods for controlling abuse.

§ 4-3. General Scope of Discovery

There is a three-pronged approach to *what* is discoverable. Civil litigants may discover information which is not privileged, relevant to the subject matter, and either admissible or reasonably calculated to lead to admissible trial evidence. CCP §2017(a).

The next two sections of this Nutshell address the first of these three prongs - that is, privileged and privilege-related matter (work product).

§ 4-4. Privilege

Certain evidentiary privileges restrict the availability of important information at both the pre-trial discovery and trial phases. The degree of protection from disclosure is greater than that of some "lesser" privileges, which must often give way to the need to know.

The attorney-client privilege, for example, is an "absolute" privilege, designed to shield the private conversations of lawyer and client. Such discussions are normally undiscoverable, either before or during trial. A number of evidentiary privileges, however, *may* be penetrated. Consider the case of a manufacturer's modification, after a personal injury suit is filed which alleges a design defect in its product. Evidence Code § 1151 prohibits the introduction of that subsequent remedial change at trial. The jury will, too readily, construe the change as an admission of liability. This general insulation from disclosure may be penetrated, however, at the discovery stage (or in some cases, at trial).

There are two reasons for piercing such a privilege at the pre-trial stage. First, *knowledge* of a dangerous condition is not privileged information. It should not be cloaked with the protective shield of the subsequent remedial repair privilege. Pre-trial discovery of such knowledge, at a stage where there is no jury present, thus cannot mislead a jury who might otherwise misinterpret the fact of repair to establish liability. The related reason for piercing this privilege during discovery is the absence of a jury at this stage of the case. The trier of fact is not privy to the manufacturer's discovery response admitting the modification - but not liability.

§ 4-5. Work Product

Work product is material prepared in anticipation of litigation. It includes documents containing the attorney's impressions, conclusions, opinions, or legal research. It is also material gathered by other persons, retained by the attorney on behalf of the client. Examples include reports made for an attorney by investigators or consultants, who have been hired to share their expertise with that lawyer in anticipation of litigation.

Attorney work product is the most pervasive problem with discovery limitations. It is generated in virtually all civil cases. Also, attorneys are not known for their willingness to engage in the mutual exchange of discoverable information. Thus, it is not surprising that this doctrine has occupied so much of the caselaw and literature on pre-trial discovery.

The work product exemption from discovery can be distinguished from the terms "attorney-client privilege" and "privilege."

The attorney-client privilege protects only direct communications, oral or written, between attorney and client. Work product protects much more. It encompasses all matter generated by lawyers and their agents regarding the client's litigation. Thus, the attorney-client privilege does not always provide the degree of protection afforded by the work product immunity. For example, California recognizes a crime-fraud exception to the attorney-client privilege. This exception does not apply, however, to the attorney's work product. BP Alaska Exploration, Inc. v. Superior Court (1988).

The work product immunity from discovery is also distinguishable from privileged communications. The CCP refers to work product information as "privileged."CCP §2018(f). Privileged information is traditionally protected, however, by the formal privileges contained in the California Evidence Code (or the applicable Federal Rules of Evidence in federal cases). Communications governed by such privileges is normally excluded from disclosure at the discovery and trial phases, to protect the privacy interests of the persons involved in certain confidential relationships. Work product, on the other hand, is comparatively accessible - given the various statutory bases for piercing the various categories of work product.

Why, then, is work product generally immune from discovery?

The state and federal systems loathe parasitic discovery. As succinctly stated in CCP § 2018(a):

It is the policy of the state to: (1) preserve the rights of attorneys to prepare cases for trial with that degree of privacy necessary to encourage them to prepare their cases thoroughly and to investigate not only the favorable but the unfavorable aspects of those cases; and (2) to prevent [other] attorneys from taking undue advantage of their adversary's industry and efforts.

The principal work product distinction is "absolute" versus "qualified." The United States Supreme Court's creation of the work product doctrine for the federal system distinguished - but did not clearly define - these important terms. Hickman v. Taylor (1947). Neither the FRCP nor California's subsequent codification of work product, define it.

Compared to the federal rule, the legislative expression of California's *absolute* work product rule is quite intense. CCP 2018(c) provides that any "writing that reflects an attorney's impressions, conclusions, opinions, or legal research or theories *shall not* be discoverable under *any* circumstances" (emphasis added). FRCP 26(b)(3) provides that "the court *shall protect against* disclosure of the mental impressions" and work product of the attorney (emphasis added).

The application of California's so-called "absolute" work product rule, however, is more limited than a plain meaning interpretation of CCP § 2018(c) would indicate. For example, the State Bar may discover the absolute work product of an attorney subject to disciplinary proceedings. Work product may be introduced when attorneys are engaged in fee arbitration disputes with their clients. And, there is no work product immunity for attorney impressions and conclusions, when clients sue their lawyers for malpractice. The literal language of CCP § 2018(c) thus yields, in cases where mandatory application would be inconsistent with its purpose.

The other category of work product is referred to as "qualified" work product (also labeled as conditional, finite, limited, etc.). California's statement of the qualified work product rule is broadly stated. Specifically, "the work product of an attorney is not discoverable unless the court determines that the denial of discovery will unfairly prejudice the party seeking discovery in preparing that party's claim or defense or will result in an injustice." CCP §2018(b). The comparatively limited (and lucid) federal rule provides that qualified work product is available "upon a showing of substantial need * * * and that the [requesting] party is unable without undue hardship to obtain the substantial equivalent by other means." FRCP 26(b)(3).

The state and federal rules have been applied similarly, due to the comparability of their respective "prejudice" and "substantial need" requirements. California's "injustice" basis for obtaining work product, however, is susceptible to broader application than the federal rule's "need/hardship" formulation. There is no "injustice" exception in the federal rule.

Under what circumstances is qualified work product available to an adversary? Examples include the unavailable witness who has given a written statement to only one side; or, an attempted monopolization of consultant experts. And, there may be an "injustice" which justifies such discovery. It may be socially desirable to discover an adversary's trial witness list in certain cases. Family law involves special public interest. The best interests of the child, for example, may outweigh limitations on the traditional barriers to the discovery of such work product. See In re Jeanette H. (1990).

§ 4-6. Relevance to the Subject Matter

There is a fundamental difference between "relevance" and "relevance to the subject matter." The common law standard, utilized prior to the modern development of civil discovery, did not distinguish the scope of inquiry for the trial and pre-trial stages. In either situation, one could inquire only about matters directly relevant to the issues in the pleadings. Now, one may also inquire into matters relevant to the "subject matter" at the discovery stage. This expansion is directly related to the modern purposes of discovery: efficiency, integrity of the overall judicial process, and avoidance of trial by ambush.

The outer limits of discovery are available prior to trial. There are significant limitations, however, during trial. The prominent justification for the comparatively limited scope of trial inquiry is the presence of the jury. This body is easily mislead by instantaneous questions and responses, or trial ploys to elicit inadmissible information.

Prior to trial, discovery inquiries are not as confrontational or sensitive. The lawyers are presumably aware of the uses and misuses of an adversary's pre-trial inquiries. The respective litigants can ask and answer (or object to) discovery questions, without having to gauge the impact of their actions on a jury. And, with the exception of depositions, the responding party has a comparatively great deal of time within which to frame a response or objection. Thirty days to respond to interrogatories is an eternity, compared to less than thirty seconds to object to an inadmissible question at trial.

What, then, does this comparatively broad language, relevance to the subject matter, mean? CCP § 2017a is silent. The California Supreme Court provided the basic guidance. Rather than a bright-line rule, its formulation was that no "precise or universal test of relevancy [to the subject matter] is furnished by the law. The question must be determined in each case according to the teachings of reason and judicial experience." Pacific Telephone & Telegraph Co. v. Superior Court (1970).

The classic illustration of the difference between *relevance* and relevance to the *subject matter* is the common question about insurance coverage. In a garden-variety tort action, the availability of insurance is irrelevant to trial issues (liability, damages, etc.). A defendant's ability to pay is normally not an element of the plaintiff's case. The parties may nevertheless discover the existence of insurance, the identity of the carrier, the nature and limits of coverage, and whether there is a coverage dispute between the carrier and the defendant. CCP § 2017(b).

The "subject matter" of routine auto accident cases thus includes insurance coverage. The plaintiff's attorney may be sanctioned for introducing inadmissible evidence of insurance during trial. It would border on malpractice, however, *not* to inquire into insurance coverage during the discovery stage of the same case. Pretrial insurance questions must be answered. This broadened scope of inquiry, into clearly *in*admissible matter, thus improves the efficiency and integrity of the already-burdened California court system. It effectively evacuates pointless lawsuits against judgment-proof defendants.

Due to California's flexible definition of relevance, pre-trial relevancy objections are rarely successful. As stated by the *Pacific Telephone and Telegraph* Court, "the relevance of the subject matter standard must be reasonably applied; * * * doubts as to relevance should generally be resolved in favor of permitting discovery. Given this very liberal and flexible standard of relevancy, a party attempting to show that a court abused its discretion in finding material relevant for purposes of discovery bears an extremely heavy burden."

§ 4-7. Calculated to Lead to Admissible Evidence

The final prong in the scope of discovery is as follows: something is discoverable "if the matter is itself admissible in evidence or appears reasonably calculated to lead to the discovery of admissible evidence." CCP § 2017(a). Again, the CCP does not limit discovery to the confines of the admissibility provisions of the California Evidence Code.

Assume that a deponent is asked "What was the color of the light when the defendant's car passed through the intersection?" The deponent testifies as follows: "I do not know, however, another passenger said that the color was red." At trial, this question would ask for objectionable hearsay. In pre-trial discovery, however, this otherwise inadmissible question must be answered. It will undoubtedly lead to admissible evidence. Followup deposition questions will seek the identity and location of that passenger, whose testimony *would* be admissible at trial.

Parties resisting discovery typically pose the "fishing expedition" objection to pre-trial discovery. A defendant in a paternity action, for example, may seek information regarding the plaintiff's sexual activity. This could be readily characterized as a defense ploy to harass the plaintiff, or to complicate the issues. But it might also lead to the discovery of evidence which exonerates the defendant. Although a party's scope of inquiry can be limited by the importance of the privacy interest at stake, a reasonable likelihood of discovering admissible evidence may justify pre-trial discovery.

Broad discovery was contemplated by the legislature's authorization of questions which are reasonably calculated to lead to admissible evidence. Thus, California's policy is that doubts are normally resolved in *favor* of discovery, although the "method of 'fishing' may be, in a particular case, entirely improper * * * but that itself is not an indictment of the fishing expedition *per se*" (*Greyhound*, Nutshell § 4-2). To resist such discovery, parties may seek protective orders.

§ 4-8. Methods of Discovery

There are two broad categories of discovery: formal and informal. The litigants may use informal or private discovery methods - such as contacting potential witnesses or privately acquiring matters of public record.

Formal discovery in California consists of the following six methods:

- depositions
- interrogatories
- inspection demands
- medical examinations
- requests for admissions; and
- exchange of expert witness lists.

The first five of these devices are used in the federal system. FRCP 27-36.

The following sections of the Nutshell briefly summarize the use of these devices in California, and particularly, significant differences from federal practice in the state.

§ 4-9. Interrogatories

An important difference between state and federal interrogatory practice is California's so-called Rule of 35. In *superior court* actions, attorneys are limited to thirty-five "specially prepared" interrogatories; and, any number of form interrogatories drafted by the Judicial Council. Additional interrogatories are permitted, only upon a showing of the requisite complexity or need. *Municipal court* and justice court actions are governed by California's Economical Litigation Project rules. CCP § 90-100. Attorneys are thus limited to a combination of thirty-five interrogatories, production of documents, requests for admission, and one deposition. The FRCP do not contain such specific limitations. Local federal rules, however, typically restrict the number of interrogatories to a comparable number.

The state and federal systems also differ on the availability of "continuing" discovery. If an interrogatory continues to speak - i.e., requires an update after it has been truthfully answered - it effectively requires "continuing" discovery. Neither system generally permits discovery questions to retain this continued viability.

The practical difference is as follows: in California, the asking party must normally seek updates via subsequent interrogatories which ask the same question. This typically occurs near trial, when it is important to learn about the existence of new information. See California Rule of Court 331 on supplemental interrogatories. Previously identified trial experts are the exception (see Nutshell § 4-14). In federal court, FRCP 26(e) allows *certain* interrogatories to continue to speak. The answering party must seasonably update previous answers about new lay and expert witnesses, and significant information that is - or becomes - incorrect.

§ 4-10. Depositions

There are two general categories of deposition: oral and written. The former is the rule - the latter, the exception. A deposition by written questions is convenient and sometimes required. For example, a court may require that "the deponent's testimony be taken by written, instead of oral, examination" to protect against undue burden or expense. CCP §2025(i)(6). Normally, however, a written deposition is employed as a convenient method for obtaining formal responses without the cost of actually attending the deposition. The court reporter reads the prepared questions. The deponent must spontaneously respond, as in an oral deposition.

California provides detailed requirements for audio and video-taped depositions not found in the FRCP. For example, the *area* used for recording or video-taping the deponent must be "suitably large, adequately lighted, and reasonably quiet." The "operator shall not distort the appearance or the demeanor of participants in the deposition by the use of camera or sound recording techniques." CCP § 2025(l).

The distance deponents must travel to attend depositions varies. In California, individuals may be compelled to travel seventy-five miles from their residences (regardless of where the action was filed); or, within the county where the suit is filed and within 150 miles of their residences. Corporations may be deposed within seventy-five miles of their principle executive or business office (in California); or, within the county where suit is pending and within 150 miles of that office. CCP § 2025(e).

Federal witnesses may be deposed within 100 miles of their residences, where they are employed, where they transact business, or where they are *served*. The latter provision effectively permits nationwide discovery via deposition, beyond the limits of the state wherein the action is pending, but within the above geographical limits contained in FRCP 45(d)(2). See, e.g., In re Guthrie (1984).

Another distinction between state and federal deposition practice involves the filing of discovery. Depositions (and other discovery) are no longer automatically filed with the courts in California. A deposition (or relevant portion) is routinely filed, however, when a judge must review the transcript - for example, at a pre-trial hearing regarding that deposition. In federal court, depositions are routinely filed with the court.

§ 4-11. Inspection Demands

A party may obtain discovery by demanding an inspection of documents, tangible things, land, or other property. This is the appropriate method of discovery for taking photographs, conducting testing, or obtaining samples of things or places not under control of the party who needs that type of information.

The principle object of this form of discovery is to locate physical evidence. It may then be examined by an expert. Also, this discovery method may seek access to another's land or property. Thus, a defendant can enter the plaintiff's land to determine whether or how his alleged conduct harmed the plaintiff or her property.

Inspection demands also seek documentary evidence. Business records and other writings are thus available for the resolution of questions about what actually happened, or whether someone is giving credible testimony at trial.

Documents in possession of a *non*party can be obtained only by a deposition and subpoena requesting specific documents. For example, a medical malpractice plaintiff would not use the document production device to obtain a nonparty hospital's records of treatment. This plaintiff's attorney would, instead, set the deposition of the hospital's custodian of records.

Such documents or things need not be in the actual or physical possession of the party from whom such information is sought. Demanded items may also be in their "custody or control." See CCP §2031. Assume that an inspection demand is submitted to a corporate party. It cannot casually dodge production by claiming that its corporate subsidiary (not a party to the action) has custody or control of otherwise discoverable documents or things.

The use of this device is not as limited as interrogatories or requests for admissions (see Nutshell § 4-9 on the Rule of 35). There is no specific statutory limit on the number of inspection demands. There is a limitation, however, not found in the rules governing the other discovery devices. While good cause is not required to *seek* documents and things, the party *resisting* such discovery must show "good cause" to justify a protective order limiting the scope of production. For example, discovery revealing trade secrets or customer lists may present good cause for limiting discovery to only that information specifically identified and necessary to prove the particular claim or defense.

§ 4-12. Medical Examinations

Physical and mental examinations are a more intrusive form of discovery than the other methods. To obtain either form of medical discovery, the party seeking the examination must demonstrate that the examinee's condition is in controversy and that there is good cause for the particular type of examination. The "in controversy" element is routinely satisfied when the plaintiff places his or her condition is issue, by alleging the defendant's responsibility for plaintiff's personal injuries.

In the case of *physical* examinations, the principle justification is that a plaintiff chooses his purse over his privacy by filing the lawsuit. Mutuality of discovery entitles the defendant to gauge the veracity of the alleged injuries and their permanence. The defendant's formal discovery by examination is comparable to the informal discovery undertaken by the plaintiff's own treating doctors.

Obtaining a court-ordered *mental* examination requires a stronger showing that the condition is in controversy, given the comparative degree of intrusion. While the demand for a physical examination is normally made without leave of court, a defendant must obtain leave of court for a mental examination.

The demand for a *physical* examination poses no problem under CCP § 2032(c)(2). It is unnecessary to obtain a court order in California. FRCP 35(a), in comparison, is not self-executing. A federal court "may order" a physical examination. The rules of both the state and federal systems require a court order, however, for a *mental* examination. In many cases, the parties stipulate to such discovery.

Under California law, a party may plead the mental or emotional distress associated with physical injuries, without triggering a mental examination. That party must stipulate, however, that he or she is only claiming the usual mental distress associated with a physical injury such as an automobile accident. The adverse party must then demonstrate exceptional circumstances to obtain a mental examination in this instance. CCP § 2032(d).

The condition of a party, *other* than the plaintiff, may be placed in issue by the pleadings. While CCP § 2032 refers to "any" party, its language arguably contemplates only examinations of "plaintiffs" or cross-complainants who countersue, seeking damages for personal injuries from the original plaintiff (cross-defendant). The "defendant's" condition would thus be in controversy. FRCP 35 is not this specific. Federal caselaw grudgingly permits physical and mental examinations of an *original* defendant. See Schlagenhauf v. Holder (1964).

The "good cause" requirement for procuring a medical examination incorporates three distinct concerns. First, an examination cannot utilize any diagnostic test that is "painful, protracted, or intrusive." Second, a court order is required (absent stipulation), when conducting such examinations more than seventy-five miles from the examinee's residence. Third, the demand must identify the "time, place, manner, conditions, scope and nature of the examination * * * as well as the specialty, if any, of the physician who will perform the examination." CCP §2032(c)(2).

May counsel attend such examinations? There is a statutory right to counsel at a *physical* examination in California. Federal caselaw generally excludes counsel from either mental or physical examinations.

Mental examinations are another matter. The prevalent argument *against* counsel's presence is the need for an environment free of stimuli which interfere with the physician's conduct of a mental examination. The argument in *favor* of counsel's presence (i.e., the basis for seeking a protective order allowing counsel to attend) is the need to protect the plaintiff from abuse, or an examiner's questions beyond the limited scope of a proper mental examination. Edwards v. Superior Court (1976).

§ 4-13. Request for Admissions

Requests for admissions (RFA) are also subject to California's "Rule of 35" (see Nutshell § 4-9). This the least used, and most misunderstood, discovery device.

The RFA differs from the other discovery devices in several ways. First, the RFA is not designed to *elicit* information. Its mission is to take matters out of issue. If, for example, the genuineness of a document is not an issue in the particular case, then the party wishing to introduce it at trial can request that the other side admit its genuineness. This device thus promotes judicial economy and cost efficiency.

The second unique feature of the RFA is that a denial, when one should have admitted the request, can result in cost-shifting. Failure to admit the genuineness of a document, for example, may result in the proponent having to prove its authenticity at trial. If the authenticity *should* have been admitted during pre-trial discovery, the judge will require the party failing to admit to pay the proponent's related costs of proof - including the expenses and attorney's fees. CCP §2033(o).

The third distinguishing feature of the RFA is the effect of failure to respond. Courts typically impose monetary sanctions for failure to appear at a deposition or failure to respond to interrogatories. When a party fails to respond to RFAs, however, the sanction may be very different. The requests may be deemed admitted. This sanction can effectively preclude trial, or serve as the basis for a partial or complete summary judgment.

There is a critical distinction between state and federal practice, spawned by the procedure to remedy failures to respond. In California, the burden is on the *requesting* party to file a motion, seeking a court order deeming the requested matters to be admitted. In California federal courts, however, the requests are automatically deemed admitted. The burden is on the *responding* party to file a motion seeking to absolve her failure to timely respond -thus allowing the filing of late responses.

Assume that a defendant fails to respond to plaintiff's RFA. Under state procedure, the plaintiff must make the motion, asking that the court deem the unanswered requests admitted. Under federal procedure, the requests are already deemed admitted by the defendant's failure to respond. The defendant must thus move the court for an order relieving her failure to respond to the RFA. California abandoned this federal approach (automatic admissions) in its 1986 Discovery Act.

§ 4-14. Discovery of Experts

There are two categories of experts for the purpose of discovery: consultants and trial experts.

Information known or generated by consultants (also referred to as discovery experts, retained experts, undesignated experts, etc.) cannot be discovered, absent special circumstances. The work product immunity protects against discovery of their reports or oral deposition testimony (see Nutshell § 4-5).

The other category of expert is the "trial" expert. This brand of expert is initially retained in anticipation of litigation. He or she is then expressly designated as a party's expert, for the purpose of giving trial testimony favorable to the retaining party. Thus, the basic difference between a consultant and a trial expert is that the retaining attorney waives work product immunity by expressly *designating* that consultant as the client's expert for purposes of trial.

In state court, the parties simultaneously exchange information about their respective trial experts via a CCP § 2034 demand. The exchanged information includes a list containing the name and address of the expert(s), discoverable reports and writings, a statement of qualifications, and a narrative statement of the general substance of the intended testimony.

In federal court, the same expert information is obtained via interrogatories, instead of an exchange of expert witness lists. And, unlike California, experts in federal litigation cannot be deposed absent a court order (or stipulation).

One similarity is that the retaining party must timely supplement the California list exchange (CCP § 2034k) and the federal interrogatory answers (FRCP 26e(1)(b)). In appropriate circumstances, a party may augment a previously submitted list by adding another expert, withdrawing an expert, or substituting a different expert.

An adversary's compensation of the other party's expert is governed by statute. The party seeking the deposition of an expert must tender payment of the expert's fee, prior to the deposition. The fee "shall not exceed the fee charged the party who retained the expert. CCP § 2034(i). An expert may charge a higher fee for deposition testimony than that charged her client for investigative work. Rancho Bernardo v. Superior Court (1992).

§ 4-15. Sanctions in General

California's initial 1956 Discovery Act, and the 1986 revision, both base the operation of discovery on a private model. Like the federal system, state legislators have placed California discovery primarily in the hands of the private parties to the lawsuit. Both systems thus operate on the assumption that the respective lawyers are familiar with the relevant statutory provisions, applicable caselaw, and other available information - enabling them to conduct discovery *without* judicial assistance.

Discovery is supposed to be self-executing. Yet, there are failures in the system, often resulting from the tension between a self-perpetuating design and an adversarial process. When a discovery dispute arises, the parties resort to the courts for assistance. This assistance takes the form of a pre-trial ruling, and, applicable sanctions for misuse (or nonuse) of the discovery process.

There is a significant difference between California and federal judicial control of discovery. In California, discovery sanctions are used to return the aggrieved party to the position she would have occupied - had the recalcitrant party not evaded his discovery obligations.

Federal decisions permit discovery sanctions for the additional purpose of punishment, contrary to the California precedent. California has not yet adopted this "punitive" approach to discovery sanctions.

In 1976, the U.S. Supreme Court announced the new deterrence orientation for federal sanction orders. Federal trial judges were instructed to divest their traditional reluctance to use the most drastic sanctions. They were instructed to impose such sanctions, when appropriate, to send a message to other litigants which would deter them from similar discovery abuses. National Hockey League v. Metropolitan Hockey Club (1976).

§ 4-16. Discovery Oversight

What *is* sanctionable conduct in California, and what types of sanctions do judges impose?

The 1986 Discovery Act instituted an expandable shopping list of discovery abuses. The CCP § 2023 "misuses" of the discovery process include:

- persistent attempts to obtain information beyond the scope of discovery;
- failing to use the proper procedure for a particular discovery method;
- causing unwarranted annoyance, embarrassment, oppression, burden, or expense;

- failing to respond;

- unjustified objections;

- evasive responses;

- disobeying a court order;

- unjustified motions to compel or limit discovery; and,

- failing to confer with the opposing party, to attempt an informal resolution of a discovery dispute.

That code section's related sanctions for the listed abuses of the discovery process include:

- monetary sanctions (imposable on the client or the attorney);

- establishment/preclusion orders, which remove issues from the case;

- precluding trial testimony for failures to comply with discovery obligations;

- termination of the lawsuit; and,

- contempt orders.

California's 1986 Discovery Act departed from the federal model, which clusters the federal sanction provisions into one rule. FRCP 37. The legislature dispersed *specific* sanction provisions throughout the Act. CCP § 2016-2036. In addition to the above-listed general "misuses" of discovery (contained in CCP § 2023),

California's individual code sections - governing each discovery method - also contain device-specific sanctions.

The integration of discovery methods and related sanctions thus clarifies questions about what sanctions are appropriate under what specific conditions. Suppose, for example, that a party appears for a deposition but does not cooperate. He refuses to properly testify. This can be a situation involving either no testimony or evasive answers. An unjustified failure to proceed with the deposition must be monetarily sanctioned under the code section on deposition procedure. CCP §2025. Failure to obey a subsequent court order to proceed will result in imposition of any of the array of sanctions incorporated from the general sanctions statute. CCP § 2023.

§ 4-17. Subjective v. Objective Standards

In addition to the device specific santions under the Discovery Act, attorneys and their clients may be sanctioned for tactics which are frivolous or intended to cause delay. The California and federal courts do not use the same standard for assessing whether to impose these sanctions.

California's 1986 Discovery Act is equivocal about which standard applies. The federal rule is quite clear.

CCP § 128.5 apparently applies a combined objective "frivolous" and subjective "bad-faith" standard to pleadings (see Nutshell § 3-10). A showing that a discovery tactic was totally without merit does not settle the issue of whether there has been a "bad faith" abuse. The lack of merit certainly suggests bad faith. It is not, however, the exclusive inquiry under the CCP.

For purposes of discovery, CCP § 128.5 should thus be compared to FRCP 26(g). That federal rule is based exclusively on an objective standard (like Rule 11 at the pleading stage). Federal sanctions are thus based on a showing that no reasonable attorney would have conducted discovery in the manner undertaken by the attorney (or client) whose conduct is in question.

§ 4-18. Discovery of Punitive Damages

In California, punitive damages may not be discovered unless they are in issue, and sought under the conditions now imposed by the Civil Code and the Code of Civil Procedure. Defendants are understandably concerned about their personal assets becoming a matter of public record. To discover such assets (other than insurance coverage), plaintiffs could merely plead an intentional cause of action supporting the imposition of punitive damages under the substantive law of California. The 1987 Brown-Lockyer Civil Liability Reform Act addressed justified complaints about fishing expeditions into the net worth of the defendant. The effect of that Act, pleading requirements, and related statutory amendments are set forth below.

When punitive damages are alleged, defendants may routinely obtain protective orders requiring plaintiffs to prove a prima facie case of liability for such damages, *prior* to introducing evidence on this issue. Plaintiffs cannot conduct pre-trial discovery, absent a court order permitting such discovery. Civil Code § 3295.

There is an additional limitation imposed on plaintiffs who want punitive damages from health care service providers. In these professional negligence cases, a plaintiff may not even *allege* punitive damages in the initial complaint. They must file a subsequent motion, seeking an amendment allowing them to plead punitive damages against doctors, hospitals, etc. The plaintiff must therein establish, through supporting affidavits, a "substantial probability that the plaintiff will prevail on the claim pursuant to Section 3294 of the Civil Code." CCP § 425.13. Civil Code § 3294 permits punitive damages only in cases where the defendant has been guilty of fraud or oppression as a result of homicide or other "despicable" conduct.

It is not clear whether California's procedural limitations on the pleading and discovery of punitive damages apply in actions filed in California's federal courts. Punitive damages have long been a part of the federal common law. The array of recent U.S. Supreme Court cases dealing with this subject rejected constitutional attacks on the absence of standards for determining the *amount* of punitive damages.

CHAPTER V

DISPOSITION WITHOUT TRIAL

§ 5-1. Introduction

The introductory course in federal civil procedure heavily emphasizes pre-trial dispositions, whereby the case is quickly ushered out of the federal system due to some jurisdictional or venue defect. Such dispositions are not the standard fare of California practice. The bulk of California's dispositions before trial arise in a variety of contexts which are not covered in the first-year procedure course. These will be addressed in the following sections of this chapter of the Nutshell. Dispositions related to demurrers without leave to amend, discovery sanctions, or lack of diligent prosecution are covered in other chapters of this Nutshell.

§ 5-2. Summary Judgment Generally

California's motion for summary judgment disposes of an entire case, or part of a case, when either the cause of action or defense has no merit. This motion is granted when the supporting materials demonstrate the absence of a "triable issue as to any material fact and that the moving party is entitled to a judgment as a matter of law." CCP § 437(c).

105

A summary judgment motion is typically accompanied by affidavits, relevant discovery, and any matters of which the court can take judicial notice. The information contained in supporting and opposing affidavits must be based on personal knowledge and admissible evidence. It must demonstrate the affiant's competence to testify on the particular matter addressed by the motion.

The basic function of this motion is to screen certain cases from the system, after they are at issue and before trial. Many cases survive the initial pleading stage, where a demurrer tests only whether the plaintiff has presented a complete and viable *prima facie* statement. Nonsuits and directed verdicts attack the merits of a weak case at the trial stage. In the interim, summary judgment exposes those cases wherein discovery reveals the absence of a genuine or winnable case.

§ 5-3. Summary Judgment Timelines

There are several differences between summary judgment procedures, and those procedures which apply to other California motions. Some important examples are minimum notice requirements, mailing provisions, and how soon (or late) this motion can be made.

The minimum time for providing notice of this motion (and responsive papers) is longer than most motions. California motions must generally be filed and served no later than fifteen "calendar" days prior to the hearing (see Nutshell § 3-13). The minimum notice period for summary judgment motions, however, is twenty-eight days prior to the hearing. Opposition papers are due fourteen days prior to the hearing (rather than five days).

California's summary judgment timelines vary from the federal rules. Ten days is sufficient notice under FRCP 56(c). Opposing papers may be served one day prior to the hearing, although the local rules of California's federal courts may enlarge this period (e.g., fourteen days in the Central District).

Unlike other motions, these timeframes for summary judgment are *not* extended by mailing. Under CCP § 1013(a), the time for acting or responding is extended by an additional five days, when papers are served by mail rather than in person. That code section is expressly inapplicable, however, to motions for summary judgment.

When a summary judgment motion may first be filed, and when it can no longer be filed, also differs from other motions. The demurrer, for example, may be filed immediately after service of the complaint. A summary judgment motion, by comparison, may not be filed prior to sixty days from the answer or other general appearance. The summary judgment cutoff date, after which it may not be filed, is earlier than other motions. Discovery motions must be heard by the fifteenth day prior to trial. Summary judgment motions, however, are heard no later than thirty days before trial.

§ 5-4. State/Federal Summary Judgment Comparison

There are two major differences between state and federal summary judgment practice: first, the comparative amenability to this motion; second, the different burdens of proof.

California is not a hospitable environment for this motion. Summary judgment is often characterized as a drastic measure. The state Supreme Court's view is that this "summary procedure is drastic and should be used with caution so that it does not become a substitute for the open trial method of determining facts." Stationers Corporation v. Dun & Bradstreet (1965).

Federal courts are far more receptive. The federal Supreme Court's view is that "[s]ummary judgment procedure is properly regarded not as a disfavored procedural shortcut, but rather as an integral part of the Federal Rules as a whole * * * ." Celotex Corporation v. Catrett (1986).

California judges tend to deny summary judgment motions in favor of the oft-cited public policy of trial on the merits. Analogous *trial* motions, such as nonsuit and directed verdict, could also be characterized as depriving a litigant of trial on the merits. These latter motions do occur, however, at the trial stage. In federal court, there is less institutional resistance to the summary judgment motion.

One reason is rooted in an historical practice difference. Unlike the traditional California practice, the same judge hears all pre-trial and trial motions in the case assigned to that judge on the filing date. Federal judges have thus been comparatively familiar with all facets of each case. Unlike the waning California practice, there is no judicial assembly-line for processing the various phases of the case.

The other major distinction between state and federal summary judgment practice is the comparative burdens of proof. In California, the moving party cannot shift the

burden of proof. Assume that Defendant's summary judgment motion attacks liability. The responding Plaintiff has
the trial burden of proof on that issue. The defendant
must demonstrate precisely how and why the plaintiff
does not have a case.

In federal court, Defendant, who does not have the trial
burden of proof, may merely make a "showing" which
suggests the absence of a factual issue. Then, Plaintiff must
respond with evidence to avoid summary judgment; that is,
evidence which would support a trial verdict in favor of
Plaintiff. As stated in *Celotex*: "the burden on the moving
party may be discharged by "showing" - that is, pointing out
to the District Court - that there is an absence of evidence to
support the nonmoving party's case."

California courts have expressly refused to follow *Celotex*.
They consider it incompatible with California summary
judgment limitations. Specifically, there is "nothing in the
statute which lessens the burden of the moving party simply
because at the trial the resisting party would have the burden
of proof * * *. In short, 'the placement of the burden of proof
at trial does not affect the showing required for a summary
judgment' in California." Biljac v. First Interstate Bank of
Oregon (1990).

§ 5-5. Judgment on the Pleadings

A party may move for judgment on the pleadings (JOP)
when the alleged defect appears on the face of the pleadings.
The court may consider only the express content of the
pleadings, and matters of which it can take judicial notice.

The moving party claims that the responding party cannot recover as a matter of law. This motion is similar to a general demurrer, which also attacks the viability of the claim or defense. It differs because it may be asserted at any time during the suit - even after a demurrer is no longer timely.

A JOP motion may be made by either party. A defendant may assert that the plaintiff cannot recover under any circumstances. A governmental defendant that has not waived sovereign immunity, for example, will use this motion because the case cannot be won. Or, a defendant may have tendered an unrecognized defense - such as an "answer" which fails to either admit or deny the allegations of the complaint. Thus, the plaintiff may attack this failure to state facts sufficient to constitute a viable defense.

Unlike FRCP 12(c), the CCP does not contain this motion. It is a product of California caselaw.

§ 5-6. Default Judgments

A default judgment may occur in one of two situations: (1) the defendant is properly served, but ignores the complaint; or, (2) either party fails to comply with litigation obligations.

The first scenario is the more common form - a "true" default. It occurs at the inception of the lawsuit. Assume that a properly served defendant fails to answer the complaint. A California plaintiff then proceeds as follows. In contract actions, the plaintiff files a written application requesting the clerk (or judge) to *enter the default* in the court's records. The plaintiff then applies for a judgment, based on this initial stage of the default process. The defendant then looses the right to defend on the merits, and may move to set aside the default or subsequent default judgment. In contract actions, the clerk enters a *default judgment* in the amount stated in the pleadings. There is no need for a hearing. In other actions, however, the plaintiff must also "prove up" his or her damages at a hearing, in order to obtain a judgment. CCP § 585.

The plaintiff must provide proper notice of damages. This presents a common problem in non-contractual default cases. Under CCP § 425.10(b), superior court actions for personal injury or wrongful death may *not* state the amount of damages in the complaint. Thus, the complaint *cannot* provide a defaulting defendant with notice of the amount that plaintiff will seek at the "prove up" hearing. To present evidence at the hearing, the plaintiff must have served a separate statement of damages on the defendant, before the default can be taken. CCP § 425.11. This situation does not arise in federal court, where the amount of damages must be stated in the complaint.

The second type of default censures a party who answered, but subsequently failed to comply with litigation obligations. This form of default is typically spawned by flagrant discovery abuse. It is expressly authorized as a discovery sanction against *either* party. CCP § 2023(b).

Can a court enter this latter type of "default" judgment, in an amount *greater* than that sought in the complaint? Assume that the defendant has engaged in outrageous conduct, during the course of discovery. The court decides to "default" the defendant. For this defendant, the default strikes the answer, due to defendant's failure to comply with discovery obligations.

A defaulted defendant is supposed to be given notice of the maximum liability for his or her inactions. The fundamental question is whether the court should be free to assess damages in any amount it deems just when the default is based on a striken answer.

When proving up damages, plaintiffs must state the desired amount of damages in either (a) the prayer of the complaint, or, (b) the statement of damages notice under CCP § 425.11 (superior court personal injury or wrongful death actions). In either event, they must subsequently present notice of their intent to seek an amount greater than previously indicated. Thus, the type of default does not affect the outcome. The plaintiff may not recover an amount greater than stated in the complaint, or special § 425.11 statement, without *amending* that complaint or statement of damages. The defendant, who is thus "defaulted" after she has answered the original complaint, may then answer the amended complaint. She thus avoids the initial "default." Greenup v. Rodman (1986).

§ 5-7. Federal Default Comparison

There are two prominent differences in state and federal default procedure.

The first distinction is that a California plaintiff's "prove up" hearing is typically ex parte. Federal procedure provides for a contested minitrial, on the sole issue of damages for a default judgments.

Second, California default judgments cannot exceed the amount of the prayer. Caselaw does not distinguish between defaults where there is a failure to answer, and defaults imposed for failure to comply with litigation obligations (*Greenup*). In a minority of federal courts, this across-the-board limitation does not apply to defaults for failure to comply with litigation obligations. A plaintiff may thus obtain an amount greater than stated in the complaint. The Ninth Circuit, however, currently applies the majority rule which does not make this distinction. Fong v. United States (1962).

§ 5-8. Offer of Judgment

California public policy encourages the settlement of cases. Otherwise, every county's civil backlog would be unmanageable. To promote settlement, there is a statutory procedure which creates a significant incentive to settle. When a case is not settled, after a *statutory* offer, parties who should have settled may prevail at trial. Yet, they may be liable for the losing party's costs and certain fees. This is the so-called "Section 998 offer."

Assume that the defendant's attorney offers $30,000.00 to settle a case with the plaintiff's attorney (orally, or in writing). This offer will have no bearing on the case, beyond plaintiff's decision whether or not to accept. If the same offer is a written CCP § 998 offer, however, there is much more to consider.

Assume that Plaintiff rejects that offer, and wins at trial. Plaintiff obtains a judgment for $25,000.00. Plaintiff, although successful, may nevertheless incur four adverse consequences. First, Plaintiff cannot recover costs immediately after the offer, otherwise obtainable by the prevailing party. Second, Plaintiff must pay Defendant's costs - from the time of the statutory offer. Third, the court has the discretion to require Plaintiff to pay Defendant's costs - also from the time of the *filing* of the complaint. Finally, this discretion extends to Defendant's expert witness fees, necessary to prepare for and proceed with trial.

There is a limitation which curbs abuses. Section 998 offers must be reasonable. For example, Defendant's $1.00 offer at the inception of a lawsuit is unlikely to trigger the trial court's discretion to award costs or fees for a defense judgment.

§ 5-9. Federal Offer of Judgment Practice Distinguished

There are three major differences in state and federal offer of judgment practice in California. They are (1) who may make such offers; (2) revocability; and (3) the applicability of this device, in the event of a defense judgment.

Under California practice, *either* party may make a § 998 offer of judgment. A plaintiff may thus make this statutory offer, as well as the defendant. Federal plaintiffs may *not* make such offers of judgment. Only "a party defending against a claim" may make such an offer (FRCP 68). This includes plaintiffs who are defending counterclaims.

Revocability of the offer varies under state and federal procedure. California offers are revocable. T.M. Cobb v. Superior Court (1984). Federal Rule offers are irrevocable.

One could argue that California should follow the federal rule of irrevocability. As the *Cobb* dissent contends:

> It is apparent that if the offeror is permitted to revoke the offer within the statutory time and before acceptance, the [statutory policy encouraging] settlement will be defeated. The settlement period established by the Legislature is short and provides an offeree a reasonable period to cogitate and make a decision. If the offer is permitted to be revoked before an adequate time has passed to consider and respond to the offer, the legislative policy of encouraging settlements is frustrated.

California nevertheless applies the standard contract principle - that an offer may be withdrawn at any time prior to acceptance. The comparative length of the state rule (thirty days versus ten days) arguably warrants the federal rule of irrevocability. One supporting theory is that new developments are more likely to occur during the longer California statutory period, which is three times longer than the federal period during which a Rule 68 offer remains open.

The third procedural difference is the applicability of this device to defense judgments. Assume that Defendant makes a statutory offer. Plaintiff refuses. At trial, Plaintiff does not obtain "fewer" dollars than offered; rather, Plaintiff obtains *nothing*. Section 998 still applies. There is no legal distinction between Plaintiff's obtaining fewer rather than no dollars. FRCP 68 does not apply in this situation. It only applies to judgments "obtained by" Plaintiff. Thus, a federal offer of judgment is vitiated by a defense judgment - although Plaintiff received less than offered.

§ 5-10. Contribution

There is a right of contribution among tortfeasors or contract obligors. It is triggered when one of them pays the entire judgment rendered against all of them, or more than that defendant's share of the judgment. Where each defendant is liable for the entire amount of the judgment, a defendant who pays it thus has a right to sue the other defendant for contribution. (This right does not apply to non-economic damages, where each defendant is liable only for his or her portion of the overall liability).

A defendant who settles prior to judgment is, of course, released from further liability to the *plaintiff.* But what impact does such a settlement have on the right to contribution? Settling defendants obviously want to be discharged from liability for any subsequent contribution to the defendants who go to trial, rather than settle.

Under former California law, a defendant who settled prior to judgment, had no obligation to consider the comparative liability of the other defendants - who chose trial over settlement. That rule promoted the public policy favoring settlement without limitation.

The Legislature imposed some limitations in CCP §§ 875-877.6, however. A pre-trial settlement, of course, reduces the claims against the other defendants (who go to trial) in the amount stipulated by the release. The right of contribution must be administered in accordance with the principles of equity. Thus, a plaintiff's release of less than all defendants must be given in "good faith." There must be a hearing on the specific issue of the adequacy of the proposed settlement, to insulate the settling defendant from further liability for contribution to the co-defendants.

What is a *good faith* settlement - in other words, one which will relieve a settling defendant from any liability for contribution to the nonsettling defendants? The reasonableness of the proposed settlement hinges on a number of objective factors. As stated by the California Supreme Court, the § 877.6 good faith hearing must take into account:

> a rough approximation of plaintiffs' total recovery and the settlors' proportionate liability, the amount paid in settlement, the allocation of settlement proceeds among the plaintiffs, and the recognition that the settlor should pay less in settlement than he would if he were found liable after trial * * * [and the] settlement figure must not be grossly disproportionate to what a reasonable person, at the time of settlement, would estimate the settling defendant's liability to be. Tech-Bilt v. Woodward-Clyde & Associates (1985).

§ 5-11. Federal Contribution in California

There is no general federal right to contribution. Where there *is* a statutory right to contribution, federal judges must, of course, apply the statute. Federal statutes are typically silent, however, about *whether* there is a right to contribution among tortfeasors. And, there is no federal statute to consider in diversity cases. Federal judges are thus asked to decide whether the underlying federal interests permit them to fashion a right to contribution as a matter of federal common law. Texas Industries v. Radcliff Materials (1981). In these circumstances, they may resort to the law of the state in which they sit.

The Ninth Circuit looks to California practice but does not follow it completely. There is a similar hearing, to determine the appropriateness of the settlement. The result is a federal "bar order" - meaning that other defendants are barred from seeking further contribution from the defendant who has properly settled.

Federal practice differs in two interrelated ways. First, the jury determines the relative culpability of the defendants, *including* the settling defendant. Second, the nonsettling defendants pay only their proportionate shares of the federal judgment. Unlike California practice, they do not have to pay the entire amount of the judgment (offset only by the amount of the settlement). Franklin v. Kaypro (1989).

Assume that plaintiff A sues defendants B, C, and D. B pays A $10,000.00 in a pre-trial settlement. That settlement is approved at either a California good faith hearing or by a federal bar order. Assume further that the (federal) jury determines that B, C, and D were each responsible for one-third of A's damages. A's trial verdict is $100,000.00.

There is a significant difference in the amount of the judgment that plaintiff A will actually recover. In state court, $10,000.00 will be offset from the total verdict, prior to C and D paying the remaining $90,000.00 to satisfy the judgment. C and D thus pay the $23,000.00 discount that B saved by settling prior to trial. In California, there is no determination of B's relative culpability. for economic damages. The nonsettling parties must thus pay the amount of the $90,000.00 judgment (after offsetting the settlement amount). In federal court, C and D will *not* have to pay B's $23,000.00 discount. They do not have to pay any more than their proportional shares of liability (approximately $66,000.00).

§ 5-12. Types of Arbitration

There are three general categories of arbitration in California: Contractual, Judicial, and International. These alternative dispute resolution mechanisms avoid the time and expense associated with the traditional mode of courtroom litigation.

The Contractual Arbitration statutes (CCP § 1280-1285 & Rules of Court 1600-1617) contain procedures for implementing a contractual agreement to arbitrate. The parties may agree to arbitrate at any stage of their relationship. Once this agreement is made, however, it is enforceable or voidable like other contracts.

The CCP contains specific provisions for the orderly conduct of this private arbitration. Examples follow:

- the parties may arbitrate under the CCP, or whatever independent set of rules they choose.

- a petition to arbitrate may be filed in lieu of an answer to a complaint;

- failure to seek arbitration may constitute a waiver of the right to arbitrate;

- subpoenas may then be issued to compel the attendance of witnesses and to produce documents;

- a party may petition a court to confirm, correct, or vacate an arbitral award;

- an appeal may be taken in the same manner as provided for in ordinary civil actions.

The contractual arbitration statutes are typically used by health care service providers, construction companies, real estate companies, and an increasing number of service industries. The CCP contains specific provisions for the arbitration of medical malpractice, public construction, and real estate claims.

The California Legislature introduced Judicial Arbitration in 1978. CCP § 1141.10(a) expresses the central concern that:

The * * * litigation involving small civil claims has become so costly and complex as to make more difficult the efficient resolution of such civil claims [and] that the courts are unable to efficiently resolve the increased number of cases filed each year, and that the resulting delays and expenses deny parties their right to a timely resolution of minor civil disputes.

Several related statutory provisions activated this program:

- superior court judges may order all cases into arbitration, when they believe that the amount in controversy will not exceed $50,000.00 for each plaintiff (double the court's jurisdictional minimum);

- ordering a case into mandatory arbitration is not appealable;

- municipal court districts may adopt a mandatory arbitration program;

- there is a right to trial de novo, so as to preserve the right to jury trial;

- when a party obtains a less favorable judgment at trial, the court may treat the higher amount awarded at arbitration as if that amount had been a § 998 offer.

The term "Judicial Arbitration" is a misnomer. It is neither judicial, nor is it really arbitration. The hearing is not conducted by a judge. The right to trial de novo vitiates the finality of a true arbitration.

The third major category of California arbitration is International Commercial Arbitration, under CCP §§ 1297-1297.432. It is available when the parties' businesses are in different countries; or, the subject matter of the dispute is outside of their respective countries.

The legislation facilitating this form of arbitration was designed to circumvent two traditional barriers to international litigation: (1) state court dismissals on the ground of *forum non conveniens*; and, (2) federal court dismissals due to lack of diversity, when there are aliens on both sides of the lawsuit.

§ 5-13. Contractual and Judicial Arbitration Compared

There are a number of differences between contractual and judicial arbitration (also referred to as "court-annexed" arbitration). Due to the increasing visibility of both forms of alternative dispute resolution, a misunderstanding of some basic variations can result in forfeiture of important rights. The Judicial Arbitration Act thus provides that it shall not be construed in derogation of the contractual arbitration title of the CCP. Thus, judicial and contractual arbitration "are mutually exclusive and independent of each other." CCP § 1141.30.

The fundamental contrast is the mandatory - versus optional - nature of the decision to arbitrate. A superior court judge may decide that a filed case's amount in controversy is, in reality, under $50,000.00. The judge can thus require judicial arbitration. The parties to a dispute may opt to insert an arbitration clause in their contract. Exercising this option mandates an arbitral, rather than judicial solution. Like a judgment, the arbitrator's decision is binding - if there is no equitable basis for avoiding the contract or the arbitration clause.

The availability of discovery is one of the most practical differences between judicial and contractual arbitration. The parties enjoy full discovery rights in judicial arbitration. In contractual arbitration, discovery is available only in personal injury and wrongful death cases (absent a contrary provision in the contract).

The applicability of the California Evidence Code is another critical difference. CCP §1282.2(d) greatly relaxes the usual evidentiary requirements for presenting evidence at a contractual arbitration hearing. It provides that the "rules of evidence and rules of judicial procedure need not be observed."

For judicial arbitration, however, Rule of Court 1613(b) provides that the "rules of evidence governing civil actions apply to the conduct of the [judicial] arbitration hearing." Evidentiary relaxations include the option of presenting various written reports, documentary evidence, and witness statements to the arbitrator in lieu of live testimony. The maker of the record or witness need not be present.

California's diligent prosecution statutes present a crucial practice distinction between contractual and judicial arbitration. There is a five-year period for bringing a case to trial. Failure to do so results in a dismissal of the lawsuit (see Nutshell § 3-12). For contractual arbitration, this five-year period starts on the date that a case is ordered into arbitration. For judicial arbitration, the dismissal period commences on the date of the filing of the complaint.

The parties' decision to arbitrate a case does not necessarily avoid a dismissal after the fifth anniversary of the filing date. The diligent prosecution period may be waived, only if the parties clearly intended to enter into contractual arbitration, rather than judicial arbitration. Porreco v. Red Top RV Center (1989).

The type of arbitration also determines the availability of a trial de novo (TDN). TDN means that the whole case is retried, as if there had been no previous resolution between the parties. TDN is a constitutionally required option, when a decision has been rendered under judicial arbitration. While a party cannot control whether the case is ordered into arbitration, that party may avoid the result by demanding a trial (subject to the CCP § 998 consequences discussed in Nutshell § 5-8). The parties to contractual arbitration typically agree to binding arbitration. And, unlike the Judicial Arbitration Statute, there is no express right to a TDN under the Contractual Arbitration Statute. Parties thus agree to waive their right to jury. Subsequently, they may not seek a TDN.

Who pays the cost of the arbitration also differs. Judicial arbitration is conducted at public expense. This form of arbitration is forced onto the parties. In private contractual arbitration, however, the parties bear the cost of the proceedings. They have decided, voluntarily, to resolve their dispute outside of the public judicial arena.

§ 5-14. Federal Preemption?

The Federal Arbitration Act (FAA) co-exists with the state arbitration statutes of California. Does federal arbitration law preclude a state or federal judge from applying the California arbitration statutes?

The FAA does not mandate the arbitration of all claims within its reach. It does enforce privately negotiated arbitration agreements, when the parties expressly choose the Act as their governing law. The FAA contains no express rule on preemption, nor does it suggest a congressional intent to occupy the field of arbitration. Thus, there is no federal policy that favors arbitration under a particular set of rules.

Suppose, for example, that the parties reside in different states. Their contract involves interstate commerce, thus triggering the potential applicability of the FAA. They include the "law of the place where the work project is located" as their choice-of-law clause. It is thus unclear whether the parties have referred to state or federal law. Either California's contractual arbitration statute or the FAA could apply.

The practical difference is that, unlike the federal Act, the California statute contains a stay of arbitration provision. As stated by the federal Supreme Court: "the FAA does not require parties to arbitrate when they have not agreed to do so * * *, nor does it prevent parties who do agree to arbitrate from excluding certain claims from the scope of their arbitration agreement. It simply requires courts to enforce privately negotiated agreements to arbitrate, like other contracts, in accordance with their terms." Volt Information Sciences v. Stanford University (1989).

§ 5-15. Fast Track Disposition

The 1986 Trial Delay Reduction Act, or "Fast Track" program, is designed to minimize the delay in bringing cases to trial. During recent decades, most California counties experienced a civil case backlog of three to five years (or more) from date of filing to disposition. Fast Track is the California remedy for reducing that delay. The basic legislative and judicial provisions are contained in California

Government Code §§68600-68619 and California Rules of Court 1901-1915.

The term *Fast Track* dovetails with the fundamental goals of this delay reduction program, as summarized in California Rule of Court 1902(c):

> The goal of the court shall be to process general civil cases from filing to disposition as follows: (1) within 12 months, dispose of 90 percent, (2) within 18 months, dispose of 98 percent, (3) within 24 months, dispose of 100 percent.

The fundamental Fast Track philosophy is observable from the following two directives. The Legislature directed the California Judicial Council (JC) to "be guided by the principles that litigation, from commencement to resolution, should require only that time reasonably necessary for pleadings, discovery, preparation, and court events, and that any additional elapsed time is delay and should be eliminated." Gov't Code § 68603(a). In turn, the JC's directive to judges is that they must "achieve a just and efficient resolution of each general civil case through active management and supervision of the pace of litigation from the date of filing through its disposition." Rule of Court 1902(b).

The Fast Track system is primarily responsibility of two specific groups: the bench, and the plaintiff's bar. The JC promulgates general rules, which judges must use in all county delay reduction programs. Every county in the state is thus responsible for developing a Fast Track program, suitable for local conditions. Each county's superior court judges must adopt their own Fast Track program, modeled after statewide guidelines. Plaintiffs' attorneys must thereby complete certain acts to keep their cases on track. They must comply with the various Fast Track requirements, such as timely service on defendants and filing of at issue memorandums.

Not all civil cases are included in the Fast Track program. This system specifically excludes probate actions, guardianships, conservatorships, proceedings under the Family Law Act, juvenile court proceedings, small claims appeals, and civil petitions including writs, temporary restraining orders, receivers, lien releases, and name changes.

There are several other situations not covered by the Fast Track program for *superior* courts. Complex cases are excluded. Each delay reduction court is responsible, however, for establishing a case differentiation classification system to clarify which cases are considered "complex." *Municipal* court Fast Track is currently optional. Certain appellate courts have established voluntary Fast Track system.

The trend in California county Fast Track systems is expansion by including a greater variety of cases, as they develop experience with this system - which required all counties to implement a local Fast Track program by July, 1992.

Constitutional attacks on Fast Track legislation, and implementing local rules, are generally unsuccessful. Article VI § 6 of the California Constitution provides that the Judicial Council shall "adopt rules for court administration, practice and procedure, not inconsistent with statute * * * ." Fast Track deadlines are shorter than otherwise provided by statute. For example, the CCP permits service of the complaint until three years after the case is filed. Most counties have implemented a sixty-day period for service, however, in Fast Track cases.

Local Fast Track rules have thus been attacked, on the basis that they conflict with the CCP. Attorneys have argued that the various county Fast Track rules violate the California Constitution's prohibition of conflicts between local rules and legislation. The Government Code provisions, however, provide the express legislative authority for the JC, and local county courts, to impose shorter deadlines than the diligent prosecution provisions of the CCP. Laborers' International Union No. Amer. v. El Dorado Landscape Co. (1989).

What happens when a Fast Track requirement is not met? When a plaintiff's attorney does not keep a case on the "Fast Track," the superior court clerk sets a hearing. At, or prior to the hearing, the attorney must show why compliance was not feasible - such as when the defendant is out of the country, and thus difficult to serve. If the judge is not satisfied, monetary sanctions are usually imposed.

The Code of Civil Procedure and California Rules of Court contain the routine bases for imposing sanctions. CCP § 575.2 addresses violations of local rules, and contains the full panoply of sanctions. The Fast Track rules specifically provide that judges may dismiss, if less severe sanctions would be ineffective. Government Code §68609(d). It limits the court's power, however, by the express legislative intent to impose sanctions on the *attorney*, when the client is not at fault. Counsel's repeated failure to follow the rules, however, will not necessarily insulate the client from a *dismissal*. Intel v. USAIR (1991). The court must give notice to counsel, if it is considering a *dismissal* sanction. Moyal v. Lanphear (1989).

CCP § 177.5 addresses the *inherent* power of courts to control their proceedings via sanctions. Rule of Court 227 adds that local rule violations are also sanctionable, by imposing attorney's fees and altering the calendar status of the case. Thus, there is a comprehensive statewide scheme for regulating Fast Track sanctions.

Congress implemented a four-year pilot project in 1991, containing Fast Track principles. The Judicial Conference of the United States, and selected federal district courts (Southern District - California), are thus developing civil delay reduction plans. See Civil Justice Reform Act, 28 USC § 471.

CHAPTER VI

TRIAL

§ 6-1. What is a Trial?

Under California Evidence Code § 12, a "trial is commenced when the first witness is sworn or the first exhibit is admitted into evidence and [trial] is terminated when the issue upon which such evidence is received is submitted to the trier of fact." Neither this, nor any other California code section, defines the term *trial*.

The judicial definition is customarily drawn from City of Pasadena v. Superior Court (1931):

The courts of this state have frequently approved, in substance, the following definition of a 'trial' * * *: 'A trial is the examination before a competent tribunal, according to the law of the land, of the facts or law put in issue in a cause for the purpose of determining such issue. When a court hears and determines any issue of fact or of law for the purpose of determining the rights of the parties, it may be considered a trial.'

The application of this definition varies, depending upon the purpose of the particular statute being analyzed. This section of the Nutshell illustrates the definitional problems with the term "trial," as drawn from various California appellate analyses.

Example 1. Wife seeks post-trial enforcement of a support judgment. She files and obtains a writ of execution for claimed arrearages in Husband's child and spousal support obligations. Husband files a successful motion to quash the writ. There has been no "complaint" and no "answer" in this enforcement proceeding. Was it a "trial," thus making a new trial the appropriate relief for Wife's review of the order quashing the writ? Yes.

Wife's writ and Husband's motion to quash did not present garden-variety pleadings for the court's consideration. Yet, there was a decision on the merits of an opposing claim and defense, reached after presentation of evidence and legal argument. The enforcement proceedings thus constituted a "trial," for the purpose of reconsidering the result via a new trial motion.

Example 2. A demurrer is sustained. The plaintiff does not refile the complaint. The CCP's diligent prosecution statute requires dismissal of cases not brought to trial within five years of filing the complaint. After that period passes, the defendant thus seeks a dismissal. Did the plaintiff effectively bring the case to "trial?" No.

The court rendered a decision, after hearing legal arguments for -and in opposition to - the demurrer. Various cases have held that a hearing on demurrer *is* a trial, when followed by a judgment of dismissal. Here, however, the plaintiff's failure to refile the complaint means that there was no trial within the meaning of the diligent prosecution statute.

Example 3. A pre-trial summary judgment is entered against the plaintiff. It is reversed on appeal. The defendant now moves to dismiss, claiming plaintiff's failure to bring this case to trial within the relevant statutory period. Was the case "brought to trial," for purposes of the diligent prosecution statute? Yes.

This scenario differs from Example 2 above - there is no "trial," when a ruling on demurrer is reversed on appeal. A summary judgment reversal, however, is distinguishable. The demurrer attacked the pleadings. The summary judgment motion attacked the proof. Thus, there has been a trial for the purpose of the diligent prosecution statute.

Example 4. On the first day of trial, plaintiff's counsel calls only one witness, for the purpose of obtaining a continuance. The judge grants the continuance. The defendant's counsel later moves to dismiss the case, because the diligent prosecution period for bringing the case to trial has passed. Plaintiff's counsel opposes this motion, on the basis that the trial has already begun. Was there a "trial?" No.

There were opposing papers (as in Example 1 above). And, there was a judicial ruling on the continuance issue addressed by the testimony of the witness. There has not been a trial, however, for the purpose of the diligent prosecution statute. The judge merely considered the preliminary matter of *when* trial issues would first be presented for resolution by the trier of fact.

The above examples demonstrate that the term "trial" has thus been construed, both broadly and narrowly, to advance the purposes of the relevant statutory policy.

§ 6-2. Proceeding to Trial

There are a number of procedural steps for advancing a case to trial. This section thus summarizes the routine stages in the journey from filing to trial. This process is generally governed by California Rules of Court 209-226.

AT-ISSUE MEMORANDUM The mere filing of the case does not "move" it through the system. One or both attorneys must initiate this agenda, by filing an At-Issue Memorandum (AIM) with the court. The AIM is a standard form which provides essential information, including: a statement that all essential parties have been served; whether the right to jury will be invoked; and, the estimated length of trial.

CIVIL ACTIVE LIST Upon receipt of the AIM, the court then places the case on the Civil Active List. This is a list of cases, arranged by the clerk, in order of receipt of the AIMs in each civil case. Depending upon the particular court's backlog, the case is ultimately assigned to a department for trial some months or years later.

ARBITRATION STATUS CONFERENCE The judges hold periodic Judicial Arbitration Status Conferences. Under local rules, the AIM must state whether the case is suitable for arbitration. If the plaintiff has not already elected arbitration, Status Conference judges determine whether the case must first be arbitrated (see Nutshell § 5-12 on Judicial Arbitration).

PRE-TRIAL CONFERENCE The next step (for cases not in arbitration) is a Pre-trial Conference (PTC). It is not necessary, unless required by local rule. The parties may request a voluntary PTC. The conference judge determines, in the absence of a settlement, whether the case is ready to be set for trial.

TRIAL SETTING CONFERENCE The Trial Setting Conference (TSC) sets the date for trial. The court clerk forwards notice of the TSC to trial counsel. They appear at the TSC to co-ordinate when the case will be tried - often within thirty to ninety days after the TSC. If the case is ready for trial, the court may then give notice of the next case-management conference. If the case is not ready for trial, it may be stricken from the Civil Active List.

MANDATORY SETTLEMENT CONFERENCE This conference (MSC) must be held in all cases where the time estimate for trial is longer than five hours. It is normally conducted by an experienced settlement judge, within the three-week period prior to trial. Any party claiming damages must file and serve a settlement demand, and itemization of damages, prior to this conference.

Unsettled cases are then assigned for trial. On the trial date, the case must then be tried, dismissed, or continued upon a showing of good cause.

§ 6-3. Right to Jury

California's right to jury for civil cases is premised upon the *state* Constitution. Article I § 16 provides that trial "by jury is an inviolate right and shall be secured to all." Compared to the federal right to jury, California applies a relatively strict historical approach when this right is questioned. See C & K Engineering Contractors v. Amber Steel (1978).

Code of Civil Procedure § 592 also addresses the right to jury trial. It is available for cases involving the recovery of property, and in cases seeking damages for breach of contract and various other injuries. Neither this code section, nor the constitutional provision, effectively decipher the numerous interpretational dilemmas arising since their inception.

California's basic judicial approach to whether a cause is legal or equitable is: first, to determine whether there is a legislatively-created right to jury trial; and if not, then to explore the historical nature of the cause of action.

§ 6-4. Federal Right to Jury Compared

The federal right-to-jury decisions do *not* apply to state court civil actions. The conduct of private parties normally lies beyond the scope of the federal Constitution, unless there is some form of state action. Further, the Seventh Amendment right to jury (for *civil* cases) is not one of the fundamental rights guaranteed to the residents of every state under the Bill of Rights of the federal Constitution. Thus, California is free to shape its own right to jury - although the application of that right cannot violate either the state or federal constitutions. As a result, there are some important differences between state and federal practice. Some prominent distinctions are now addressed in this section of the Nutshell.

One important difference is the existence of a federal right
to jury, in cases which were historically within the province
of the equity courts. For example, there is a federal right to
jury in a shareholder's derivative action, although this is an
historically equitable claim. Ross v. Bernhard (1970).
California courts, on the other hand, look solely to the
historical treatment of the action, rather than its underlying
nature, to decide whether there is a right to a jury trial. Thus,
there is no right to jury for this type of lawsuit - which
expressly rejects *Ross*. Rankin v. Freebank (1975).

Another difference in state and federal jury practice
involves the so-called "overlap" of legal and equitable
issues. In both systems, for example, the same issue may lie
at the heart of the plaintiff's equity complaint, and, the
defendant's at-law cross-complaint for damages. Thus, a
judge and a jury would independently try the same issue of
fact, if these issues were not decided in the same action.

Under California's "equity first rule," the courts are
encouraged to resolve equity issues first, when judicial
economy suggests that impanelling a jury would result in
unnecessary time and expense. A-C Co. v. Security Pacific
(1985). Thus, California judges may first resolve the factual
issues in the equity complaint.

In federal court, however, judicial economy plays no
role - where the right to jury trial applies. The jury would
first have to decide any issue which, in this particular
manner, overlaps into law and equity. Beacon Theaters
v. Westover (1959).

Even where there is no such overlap, a California judge may still resolve *incidental* legal matters under the so-called "clean up" doctrine. Assume that the case is an historically equitable one, such as the action for an accounting. Under Dairy Queen v. Wood (1962), a federal jury must determine any at-law issue, no matter how incidental. California litigants are *not* entitled to a jury in this situation - which facilitates the public policy of preserving judicial resources. Thus, under *C & K Engineering* (Nutshell § 6-3), a complaint containing "a prayer for damages does not convert what is essentially an equitable action into one for which a jury trial would be available."

§ 6-5. Jury Waiver

One must request a jury. It is not automatically provided. The right to jury is thus waived by failing to timely ask for it. This right is triggered by providing notice, to the court and the other parties, of the intent to use the jury mode of factfinding at trial. This notice is typically asserted by checking the appropriate box on the At-Issue Memorandum.

The fundamental rules on jury waiver are found in the California Constitution and the Code of Civil Procedure. Article I § 16 of the Constitution provides that "a jury may be waived by the consent of the parties expressed as prescribed by statute." CCP § 631 provides that waiver is expressed by consent, or implied by conduct. Statutory examples of waiver include the failure to post jury fees twenty-five days prior to trial, and failing to deposit jury fees on a daily basis. This form of implied waiver does not occur in the federal system, where jury fees are not required.

A waiver is not irrevocable. Premised on the constitutional theme that trial by jury is an inviolate right, the CCP also provides for reinstating the right to jury. The party who did not originally claim the right to jury, for example, may rekindle this right by providing notice and paying the jury fees. This right may even oscillate back and forth between the parties, until final waiver by the last party permitted to assert it. The court thus has the discretion to allow trial by jury when there has been a waiver. Doubtful cases are construed against waiver. See Byram v. Superior Court (1977).

The California and federal courts differ on the viability of "inadvertent" waiver, as a basis for reinstating a jury trial. California is generally hospitable to such claims. Federal courts in California tend not to consider inadvertence a sufficient basis for restoring the right to jury. Failing to demand a ju   trial, after removal from state court to a federal court, is not a sufficient basis for reinstatement. Lewis v. Time (1983).

§ 6-6. Jury Size

The California Constitution, and the CCP, contain the fundamental rules on jury *size*. They provide that civil juries shall consist of twelve persons, or a lesser number agreed on by the parties.

The state Constitution includes an important exception for municipal and justice courts. The Legislature may provide for eight-person juries. CCP § 221 thus established experimental juries of eight persons in the municipal and justice courts of Los Angeles County. While the experiment has ended, it provided legislative momentum for jury size reductions in smaller cases.

The Constitution requires that stipulations for fewer than twelve jurors be made "in open court," a proviso not repeated in the implementing code section. Thus, these agreements are sometimes made elsewhere, orally in chambers or in correspondence. This does not comply with the constitution, due to the absence of a stipulation entered into the court's minutes while it is in session. The parties are estopped, however, from complaining after loosing a case decided by a smaller jury. Meder v. Safeway Stores (1979).

The federal Constitution is silent on jury size. The federal Supreme Court thus approved six-member civil juries. Colgrove v. Battin (1973). The Court perceived no difference in the potential result reached by six, as opposed to twelve jurors. The local rules in California's federal courts thus provide for the smaller jury size. The Court later drew the line at six jurors, however, for *criminal* cases.

§ 6-7. Jury Classifications

There are five jury terms commonly used in California:

- jury pool;

- venire;

- panel;

- petit jury; and,

- alternate jurors.

This section addresses the meaning and usage of each term.

JURY POOL The "pool" is the master list of *eligible* jurors, compiled by Jury Commissioners or other administrative personnel in each county. A computer process periodically generates a list of names, sufficient to provide the anticipated number of jurors needed for a specified period. The names are taken from voter registration lists, supplemented with the names of licensed drivers. The end result is the so-called master list. These are the persons who may be summoned to appear for jury duty.

VENIRE The "venire" is the group of prospective jurors who are summoned from this list. These individuals appear for jury duty for the assigned day or period. A number of these individuals are usually excused, or have their service postponed, due to personal hardships.

PANEL The "panel" is the group assigned to a particular court for trial. It may consist of twenty persons. CCP § 222 provides for the random selection of members of the panel to be seated for voir dire. The jury who actually tries the case will be selected from this panel.

PETIT JURY The "petit jury" is the group of (typically twelve) individuals who are the trial jurors. These are the individuals who survive the various challenges (voir dire) described in the next section of the Nutshell.

ALTERNATE JURORS "Alternate" jurors may accompany the petit jurors during trial. One or more additional jurors thus hear the case. The judge has the discretion to assign alternate jurors, or the parties may stipulate to their use. They are needed in long trials, where personal circumstances may preclude certain petit jurors from completing their term of jury service.

§ 6-8. Voir Dire

Voir dire is the preliminary phase of trial, used for the purpose of choosing the best jury. Its basic goal is to "select a fair and impartial jury." CCP § 222.5. The trial judge first examines the prospective jurors. Trial counsel then have the opportunity to continue this examination. The details of this process are addressed in California Rules of Court 228 and 516.

Voir dire was, historically, done exclusively by oral questioning. A number of courts are experimenting with written voir dire questions - to encourage greater candor in the responses from the potential jurors. Failure to accurately answer either form of questioning subjects the juror to perjury.

The judge's discretion controls the content, and the length, of counsels' examination. Improper questions include ones designed to precondition the jurors to arrive at a particular result, to indoctrinate the jury, or to pre-instruct jurors on the content of the law.

Federal voir dire is briefer than its state-court counterpart. Federal courts exercise greater control over the voir dire process, and permit far less participation by trial counsel. California voir dire, by contrast, may be conducted without the judge even being present. An experimental voir dire project in several California counties, which tracked the federal model, was repealed by Proposition 115 in 1990. As

a result, CCP §222.5 was passed, to reinstate counsel's right
to effectively control voir dire in civil cases. It is thus
unlikely that this gap between state and federal voir dire
practice will close.

§ 6-9. Jury Challenges

There are three categories of jury challenge in California.
They are challenges to the panel, challenges for cause, and
peremptory challenges.

CHALLENGING THE JURY PANEL A party may
challenge the jury panel, prior to the swearing of the petit
juror for trial. Notice must be given to the Jury Commissioner, who is entitled to legal counsel. Complaining parties
typically claim that the commissioner's selection procedures for the jury pool do not produce a representative cross-
section of the community.

The California Supreme Court cases on point are criminal
cases. On the assumption that their holdings may be applicable to civil cases, the following elements are required for
such a challenge in civil cases. First, a party must make a
prima facie showing of the systematic under-representation
of a particular group in the overall jury pool. If the selection
criteria are neutral as to race, ethnicity, sex, and religion,
then the complaining party must also demonstrate that the
commissioner's method of applying these selection criteria
is constitutionally impermissible. People v. Bell (1989).

An eligible juror may be properly excused on the basis of
undue hardship. The Jury Commissioner cannot, however,
automatically excuse potential jurors on the basis of occupa-
tional or economic hardship. This former California prac-

tice was characterized as a blanket exclusion which "however well-intentioned and however justified by prior actions of trial judges, must be counted among those tendencies which undermine and weaken the institution of jury trial." Thiel v. Southern Pac. (1946). All eligible jurors must be afforded the opportunity to be summoned for duty, giving them the possibility to serve, or to individually present their claim of undue hardship.

CHALLENGE FOR CAUSE A party may challenge a prospective juror (on the panel) for cause, as a result of the voir dire process at trial. There are three bases for such challenges under CCP § 225. They are normally presented at trial in the following order: general disqualification, implied bias, or actual bias.

First, jurors are "generally" disqualified for incapacities which would effectively render them incompetent. The loss of hearing, sight, or speech do not automatically bar a prospective juror from jury service. The court must decide whether the challenged individual is nevertheless capable of performing as a juror. The following are generally excluded from jury service: noncitizens, domiciliaries of other states, minors, and convicted felons.

Implied bias is the second basis for challenging a juror for cause. It includes the following:

- consanguinity within the fourth degree to any party, officer of a corporate party, or witness;

- a number of other relations suggesting implied bias - including being the parent, spouse, or child of a party;

- having been an attorney or client of a party within one year prior to the filing of the complaint;

- having an interest in the outcome of the suit.

Actual bias is the third basis for a challenge for cause. This form of bias is shown by any state of mind which prevents a prospective juror from acting with complete impartiality. One who expresses a dislike for a particular group or occupation, for example, should not act as a juror, when a member of that group or occupation is a party.

PEREMPTORY CHALLENGES The third major category of jury challenge is the peremptory challenge. No reason need be given for excusing jurors on this basis. Peremptory challenges are limited to six per side; and, eight per side when there is more than one party on that side of the case.

Another significant limitation on the exercise of peremptory challenges is that a party cannot exclude any juror for a legally unacceptable reason. CCP § 204 thus provides that "No eligible person shall be exempt from service as a trial juror by reason of occupation, race, color, religion, sex, national origin, or economic status." A trial court's failure to carefully evaluate a prosecutor's explanations for peremptory challenges to a cognizable group is constitutional error. People v. Fuentes (1991).

The typical breach is demonstrated by the exclusion of jurors based on race. The composition of both the jury pool and the petit jury must comply with the California Supreme Court cases which prohibit this practice in criminal cases. One California appellate court extended this constitutional

protection to civil cases, a decade prior to the federal
Supreme Court did so. See Holley v. J & S Sweeping (1981)
(California) and Edmonson v. Leesville Concrete (1991).

§ 6-10. Order of Trial Proceedings

After the petit jury is selected, the trial normally proceeds
as indicated in this section of the Nutshell. Some stages are
unnecessary for bench trials (opening, closing, and instructions).

OPENING STATEMENT   The opening statement informs the jury about the general nature of the claims and
defenses. The plaintiff makes the (optional) opening statement. The defendant may then open. Defense counsel often
delay their opening statement until the plaintiff rests.

PRESENTATION OF EVIDENCE   The plaintiff then
produces oral and documentary evidence during the plaintiff's
case-in-chief.   The defendant may cross-examine the
plaintiff's witnesses during this phase. The defendant then
offers evidence to establish the defense. The plaintiff may
then cross-examine defense witnesses.

REBUTTAL   The parties may offer rebuttal evidence.
This evidence is typically appropriate *after* (a) the proponent
has completed his or her case-in-chief, and (b) new matters
which have been raised during the adversary's ensuing
presentation of evidence. The proponent may thus counter
this new evidence with rebuttal testimony to explain, counter,
or disprove the adversary's new evidence.

CLOSING ARGUMENT   The parties may then give their
closing arguments.   Trial counsel thereby organize the

evidence in a coherent manner, normally without objections. They argue the implications of the evidence on behalf of their respective clients. This is the final opportunity for the lawyers to communicate with the jury before its decision.

INSTRUCTIONS The court then instructs the jury (see Nutshell §6-12). The case is then submitted to the jury for its deliberations.

§ 6-11. Trial Motions

The six common trial motions are as follows:

- motion in limine;

- nonsuit;

- motion for judgment;

- directed verdict;

- judgment notwithstanding the verdict;

- new trial.

They are summarized in this section of the Nutshell.

MOTION IN LIMINE The motion in limine is typically based on Evidence Code § 352. It allows the trial judge to "exclude evidence if its probative value is substantially outweighed by the probability that its admission will * * * create substantial danger of undue prejudice, of confusing the issues, or of misleading the jury." Its basic role is to keep certain evidence, otherwise admissible, from the jury. It is thus claimed that the evidence, if heard by the jury, is so prejudicial that the jury cannot help but overvalue its probative impact.

Assume that a doctor is sued for medical malpractice. His license to practice is revoked prior to trial. Also, there are a number of other malpractice cases pending against him. The defense attorney will likely file a motion in limine, heard before voir dire, which attempts to convince the court that these facts should be kept from the jury. It would be argued that the jury could not objectively consider the *other* evidence in this case, because knowledge of these facts would have a disproportionate impact. Thus, the defense would argue that the court should exercise its discretion to bar any mention of these truths at trial.

Unlike other motions, this motion *may* be filed during the period - just prior to trial - when there is no discovery, so that counsel may settle or prepare for trial. This motion is often made on the first day of trial.

NONSUIT Nonsuit is a defendant's motion, made during a jury trial. It is made after the plaintiff has completed either the opening statement, or the presentation of plaintiff's evidence. CCP § 581(c). This motion is, effectively, a delayed demurrer. Rather than attacking the pleadings, it attacks the plaintiff's opening statement, or the plaintiff's case-in-chief. It concedes the truth of the facts offered. It denies, however, that plaintiff can recover under the applicable law.

This motion is not favored. When made after the opening statement, the plaintiff is normally given an opportunity to cure the claimed defect by offering additional evidence. When made after the presentation of plaintiff's evidence, it could preclude submission of the case to the jury. Thus, the California Supreme Court's views that:

> courts grant motions for nonsuit only under very limited circumstances. A trial court must not grant a motion for nonsuit if the evidence presented by the plaintiff would support a jury verdict in the plaintiff's favor. * * * Although a judgment of nonsuit must not be reversed if plaintiff's proof raises nothing more than speculation, suspicion, or conjecture, reversal is warranted if there is 'some substance to plaintiff's evidence upon which reasonable minds could differ.' Carson v. Facilities Development (1984).

MOTION FOR JUDGMENT The motion for judgment is basically the same motion as the motion for nonsuit. There are two essential differences. First, the motion for judgment is used in *bench* trials. Second, the judge *may* weigh the evidence, to determine whether plaintiff has presented substantial evidence.

DIRECTED VERDICT The directed verdict motion is a jury trial motion. It differs from nonsuits and motions for judgment in two ways. It is available to both parties, and it is normally made after all parties have completed the presentation of their trial evidence. It is similar to the nonsuit and motion for judgment because it attacks the quality of the (opposing party's) evidence, seeking to short-circuit the attempt to get the case to the jury.

JUDGMENT NOTWITHSTANDING THE VERDICT The JNOV is based on a similar claim that the opposing party has failed to present evidence that would justify a jury verdict. The court has the power to render a judgment, thus contrary to that of the jury. It is appropriately granted "whenever a motion for a directed verdict for the aggrieved party should have been granted if made." CCP § 629.

The basic difference between directed verdict (DV) and JNOV is timing. The DV motion is made after both parties rest, prior to submission of the case to the jury. The JNOV motion is made after the jury has returned its verdict.

NEW TRIAL Article VI § 13 of the California Constitution provides for a new trial when there has been a "miscarriage of justice." The CCP sets forth a more complete list of grounds for a new trial motion. Unlike DV and JNOV motions, the judge *may* weigh the evidence. Proof of some error is not enough. The claimed error must be prejudicial, as opposed to harmless.

There are two significant procedural differences between state and federal practice concerning the above motions. First, California no longer requires the DV as a condition precedent to making a motion for JNOV. In federal court, the party seeking a Renewed Motion for Judgment (formerly JNOV) must have made a Motion for Judgment (formerly Directed Verdict) at the close of all the evidence. Second, a California new trial motion may contend that the jury erred because damages were *either* too much or too little. In federal court, this motion may only claim that the damages were too high. Thus, damages may thus be reduced (remittitur), but may not be increased (additur).

The major California trial motions are compared with the federal motions in the chart below. A blank space indicates lack of an equivalent motion.

When Made	Trial Type	California	Federal
Close of P's Arg.	Jury	Nonsuit	
Close of P's Case	Jury	Nonsuit	Motion for Judgment
Close of P's Case	Bench	Motion for Judgment	Motion to Dismiss
Close of D's Case	Bench	Motion for Judgment	
Close of D's Case	Jury	Directed Verdict	Motion for Judgment
Post Verdict	Jury	JNOV	Motion for Judgment
Post Verdict	Jury & Bench	New Trial	New Trial

§ 6-12. Instructions

The judge "charges" or instructs the jury, after both parties rest and all trial motions are resolved. The instructions are a statement of the applicable law, to aid the jury in arriving at its verdict.

The lawyers submit proposed instructions to the trial judge, before the first witness is sworn. Prior to closing argument, they may submit additional proposed instructions on matters developed by the evidence - but not contained in the pleadings. CCP § 607.

These instructions are derived from two sources: the California Jury Instructions Civil (traditionally referred to as Book of Approved Jury Instructions or BAJI) and counsels' own personally-prepared instructions. The BAJI is a two-volume set of approved jury instructions. It is constantly updated in West's *California Reporter* case advance sheets.

California's Standards of Judicial Administration recommend that judges allow the BAJI, when requested by trial counsel. Thus, when the BAJI are given, they are rarely reversed on the basis of their case-tested wording. The Standards caution, however, that judges should not give any less consideration to instructions which are individually prepared.

Counsel often disagree about the applicability of proposed instructions, or the wording of individually-prepared instructions. Even if the BAJI are the only instructions submitted to the judge, both sides will not necessarily want the same ones read to the jury.

Assume, for example, that the pleadings contain the affirmative defenses of comparative negligence and assumption of the risk. There is virtually no trial evidence, however, which supports the giving of an instruction on the latter defense. If the defendant has apparently abandoned that defense during trial, then the plaintiff's counsel would object to the court's confusing the jury by giving a BAJI on assumption of the risk.

There are, of course, disagreements when counsel prepare their own versions of the applicable law, which they want the judge to read to the jury. Each side often tailors these statements of the law, in a way which will assist the particular client. Each proposed jury instruction must thus contain a citation of authorities. The purpose is to provide support for the particular statement of law, or its applicability to the trial evidence. Citations are unnecessary, however, for forms previously approved by the court - such as the BAJI. See Rule of Court 229.

The trial judge resolves disputes about the appropriateness of the proposed instructions. This is determined out of the presence of the jury. The judge may thus give, refuse, or modify the parties' proposed jury instructions. Alleged judicial error in the selection of instructions is the most common basis for appeals in California.

The court *may* advise jury members about the availability of instructions during their deliberations. Instructions *must* be provided, however, if the jury requests them.

§ 6-13. Verdicts

This section of the Nutshell addresses the types of verdicts, the percentage of jurors necessary for a verdict, and the contest of a verdict.

TYPES OF VERDICTS There are two types of verdict: general and special.

A general verdict means that the jury finds either for the plaintiff or defendant in general terms. Verdicts "For the Plaintiff in the amount of X dollars," or, "For the Defendant" are general verdicts.

In a special verdict, the jury must make specific findings of fact. Under CCP § 625, the jury may be required "to find a special verdict in writing, upon all, or any of the issues, and * * * if they render a general verdict, to find upon particular questions of fact * * * ." A special written verdict is required, for example, in verdicts containing punitive damages.

In a comparative negligence jurisdiction like California, a general verdict is not very useful. Both sides often claim that the other is at least partially, if not totally, at fault. And, in a multiple defendant case, the liability is not necessarily pro rata. Thus, trial counsel will submit special verdict forms, requiring the jury to specially determine the degree of the plaintiff's negligence, that of the various defendants, and whether the plaintiff's negligence contributed to his or her injuries.

PERCENTAGE NECESSARY FOR VERDICT There are specific requirements for the number of jurors who can render a verdict. Article I § 16 of the California Constitution provides that "in a civil cause three-fourths of the jury may render a verdict." *May* means that the parties can stipulate to a different number. When there is a twelve-person jury, nine of the twelve must agree on the verdict. Thus, if a poll of the jury reveals that "more than one-fourth of the jurors disagree thereto, the jury must be sent out again." CCP § 618.

The same nine jurors do not have to vote in favor of each *special* verdict. Assume that nine jurors agree that the defendants are liable. The *same* nine do not have to agree on all special verdict questions. For example, the three jurors who disagreed on the issue of negligence (that would have held for the defendant) may provide the votes necessary to apportion damages among the defendants. See Resch v. Volkswagen of America (1984).

CONTESTING VERDICTS A verdict may be contested on the basis of jury misconduct. California Evidence Code § 1150 thus provides that the loosing party may impeach a verdict by presenting evidence of "statements made, or conduct, conditions, or events * * * of such a character as is likely to have influenced the verdict improperly."

A variety of situations have resulted in a new trial on this basis, including:

- chance verdicts where the jury casts lots or dice;
- quotient verdicts, where its members agree in advance to merely divide by twelve the individuals estimates of damages;

- influential statements or conduct by courtroom personnel; and

- revelations of bias, concealed during the voir dire stage of trial.

§ 6-14. Relief from Judgment

For six months after judgment, a party may make a motion for relief from judgment. CCP § 473. Trial courts may exercise their discretion, for example, to relieve a party or attorney from orders or judgments taken against them arising out of their "mistake, inadvertence, surprise, or excusable neglect."

This motion has generated the hundreds of cases, found in West's *Annotated California Code of Civil Procedure.* Mere negligence in failing to properly plead the case, or producing sufficient evidence to oppose a motion that terminates the case, are not sufficient. The neglect must be influenced by something beyond the control of the party seeking relief.

There is no distinction, however, between excusable and inexcusable neglect - in that portion of the statute dealing with *attorney* neglect which results in a default judgment against the client. The defense attorney files an affidavit of fault to attest to "his or her mistake, inadvertence, surprise, or neglect." Thus, mere neglect will protect the client from the harshness of the traditional rule that the attorney's negligence is attributed to the client. The court must grant the motion for relief, although it may sanction the attorney rather than punishing the client. The court cannot condition this relief on the attorney's paying the assessed costs or fees. This saving device is *un*available to plaintiffs' attorneys, who quite similarly wish to invoke § 473 relief. Although their negligence has resulted in a dismissal against their client, they cannot claim the benefits of this one-way statute which favors defendants in default. Billings v. Health Plan of America (1990).

FRCP 60(b)(1) contains the identical grounds for obtaining federal relief from judgment. That rule contains two significant differences from CCP § 473 however. Relief may be sought for up to one year (rather than six months) from judgment. Further, there is no express time limitation for asserting the other Rule 60(b) bases for relief from a federal order or judgment.

CHAPTER VII

JUDGMENT-RELATED REMEDIES

§ 7-1. Introduction

The maze of procedural steps to judgment do not necessarily lead to the object of the lawsuit. Even the entry of judgment after trial is not necessarily synonymous with success.

When covered at all, the shortest chapter of the federal procedure casebooks is usually the one dealing with securing and enforcing judgments. The FRCPs often defer to the practice of the state in which the Federal District Court sits. Thus, there is a need to augment such materials with a state-specific summary of the following three questions:

- what are the provisional remedies for increasing the odds that the client will be able to preserve the status quo, pending the outcome of the dispute?

- what are the methods for collecting and enforcing the judgment?

- under what circumstances are costs and attorney's fees available to offset the cost of the litigation?

159

This chapter of the Nutshell profiles California's answers to these questions.

§ 7-2. Claim and Delivery

This provisional remedy is used to obtain tangible personal property, pending the outcome of the underlying suit. Unlike the attachment of real property, claim and delivery's writ of possession temporarily answers the question of ownership or possession of a chattel.

A plaintiff must demonstrate the following elements, when seeking this pre-trial writ: (1) the plaintiff's right to immediate possession of the property; and, (2) its wrongful detention by the defendant. CCP § 512.010. Installment contract sellers, for example, often retain title when releasing possession of the item sold to the buyer. The chattel is typically the security for the repayment of a debt. The debt is in default. The plaintiff thus files his or her claim to this personal property, now wrongfully withheld by the defendant.

§ 7-3. Attachment

Property attachments are typically issued in one of three instances: to obtain jurisdiction over property, to seek relief under the general attachment statute, or to obtain security in advance of judgment.

JURISDICTIONAL ATTACHMENT This basis for attachment is emphasized in the federal civil procedure course. Under state law, however, there are a number of restrictions which are not encountered in the earlier course. The basic guidelines follow.

Jurisdictional attachment is not available in all cases. Only *nonresident* attachment is available for any type of claim, including tort and other noncontractual claims. It is not generally available, as to all defendants. The defendant must be a nonresident *individual*. Thus, where personal jurisdiction cannot be obtained, *quasi in rem* jurisdiction can be acquired by attaching a nonresident's California property. CCP § 492.010.

Foreign corporations and partnerships, subject to statutory registration requirements, are thereby subject to the personal jurisdiction of the California courts. Failure to comply with these requirements, however, subjects such entities to nonresident attachment - as in the case of individual defendants.

California's nonresident attachment statute was drafted in the same year as the federal Supreme Court's decision in Shaffer v. Heitner (1977). That case found a Due Process infirmity with attachments where the mere presence of property alone, without more, was the exclusive basis for state-court exercises of jurisdiction over property. California's current attachments of the property of nonresidents, when unrelated to the underlying litigation, are thus subject to scrutiny under *Shaffer*.

GENERAL ATTACHMENT   The general attachment statute is available to a plaintiff who sues on a contract claim. There are a number of limitations under CCP § 483.010 et seq.:

   • the underlying claim must involve a fixed or readily ascertainable amount of at least $500.00;

- the claim cannot be secured by real property (unless it has become valueless, or has decreased in value through no fault of the creditor;

- in the case of individual defendants, the underlying suit must arise out of their conduct of a "trade, business, or profession;" and

- must obtain a bond, in the event of liability for wrongful attachment.

SECURITY ATTACHMENT The third use for attachment is to secure the availability of the property, pending the outcome of the dispute. The plaintiff must show that "great or irreparable damage" would result in the absence of such an attachment. This provisional remedy is usually obtained on an *ex parte* basis without notice to the defendant. CCP § 485.010. This procedure will satisfy Due Process, only if plaintiff can properly demonstrate a clear showing of exigent circumstances. Connecticut v. Doehr (1991).

There are limitations with this form of attachment, too. To satisfy federal due process case law, plaintiff's affidavit must unquestionably demonstrate that the debtor would conceal, impair in value, or make the attached property unavailable. Western Steel and Ship Repair v. RMI (1986).

§ 7-4. Lis Pendens

Lis pendens gives notice of a pending lawsuit affecting the title to real property. Like an attachment, a lis pendens creates a lien on the property. Unlike attachment, prior notice is generally not required.

Lis pendens is often invoked in quiet title suits, partitions of real property, eminent domain proceedings, and in specific performance suits. The plaintiff files a complaint, and then records notice of the pendency of the action in the office of the county recorder - or in the local Federal District Court. The court clerk routinely issues a certification that an *ex parte* lis pendens has been filed. The plaintiff must mail notice of the lis pendens to adverse parties. CCP § 409(a)(c).

Due to the ease of obtaining a lis pendens, there are limitations on its use. The plaintiff must first secure a bond. This asset provides a fund for the defendant to proceed against, in the event of a wrongfully filed lis pendens. The plaintiff is also liable for damages proximately caused by misuse of this device. The defendant may also remove this cloud on title by applying for a separate certification of expungement.

The primary advantage to lis pendens is the plaintiff's ability to unilaterally cloud title. The defendant must either settle, or otherwise agree with the plaintiff, to lift the lis pendens. The expungement of a lis pendens dissolves the cloud on title and does not affect subsequent transferability.

Given the potential for abuse, California's judicial policy is to restrict the availability of lis pendens. It is not designed to be an unsecured creditor's short-cut for attaching real property. As cogently stated by the Court of Appeal: "We cannot ignore as judges what we know as lawyers — that the property that is the subject of a lis pendens is sometimes made not to prevent conveyance but to coerce an opponent to settle regardless of the merits." Hilberg v. Mendrin (1989).

§ 7-5. TROs and Injunctions

FUNDAMENTAL DISTINCTIONS This section of the Nutshell addresses the two related forms of injunction rendered prior to judgment: temporary restraining orders (TRO) and preliminary injunctions.

Prior to examining the general requirements for obtaining an injunction, one must first distinguish the following terms: (a) permanent injunction versus preliminary injunction; and, (b) preliminary injunction versus TRO. These terms are often used interchangeably in the cases, although they are quite distinct.

A *permanent* injunction is a judgment providing equitable relief. Such injunctions are rendered at the close of trial of the underlying action. For example, a judgment may require the defendant to specifically perform a contract obligation, by accepting the plaintiff's purchase money and executing a deed to the plaintiff.

A *preliminary* injunction is a provisional remedy, issued pending the outcome of the trial. The plaintiff, in the above hypothetical, may obtain such an injunction immediately after filing suit. That would prevent the defendant from selling the property prior to the court's ultimate decision on whether specific performance is appropriate.

A *TRO* is, in a limited sense, a preliminary injunction. It seeks the same relief. It differs only in duration. A TRO is comparatively short-lived.

Assume that a potential defendant is cutting down trees on what plaintiff believes to be plaintiff's side of their common boundary line. The plaintiff's lawyer can immediately seek a TRO, serve it on this defendant, and thus prevent the latter from destroying more trees. Due to the exigent circumstances, the TRO is issued by the court to preserve the status quo until the judge can more fully consider the ownership dispute. Whether or not the plaintiff obtains a TRO, the court may issue a preliminary injunction (some days or weeks later), pending trial of the action. If the plaintiff is unsuccessful in convincing the judge about the need for a provisional remedy, the judge will dissolve any TRO, refuse to issue a preliminary injunction, and effectively allow the defendant to continue cutting.

GENERAL REQUIREMENTS Injunctions may be granted when it appears "that the commission or continuance of some act during the litigation would produce waste, or great or irreparable injury, to a party to the action;" and, "pecuniary compensation would not afford adequate relief." CCP § 526.

Notice is generally required for both the TRO and preliminary injunction forms of such equitable relief. In the above tree-cutting hypothetical, the plaintiff's lawyer must normally serve notice of the hearing date for both a TRO and a preliminary injunction. If circumstances dictate, the TRO may be obtained *ex parte*. If that lawyer waits until she can provide written notice, or if she cannot locate the adjacent property owner who authorized the cutting of the trees, they will be gone before the case is filed or comes to trial. This is an exigent circumstance that would warrant an *ex parte* application for a TRO.

When a TRO is first served, it usually provides initial notice of the hearing date for the preliminary injunction application. The TRO usually requires the defendant to show cause why the preliminary injunction should not be issued on the date of that hearing. The defendant may thus obtain counsel, so that both sides will have an opportunity to present their views on the need for a preliminary injunction (pending trial of the underlying claim).

There is occasional confusion about the respective availability of a preliminary injunction, claim and delivery, and an attachment. Unlike Claim and Delivery (see Nutshell § 7-2), a preliminary injunction is *un*available for the purpose of repossessing personal property. Claim and delivery's writ of possession is thus the appropriate remedy. Unlike an attachment (see Nutshell §7-3), a preliminary injunction is *un*available for the purpose of acquiring possession or ownership or real property.

The TRO and preliminary injunction are comparatively broader in scope than the other provisional remedies. The Court of Appeal in Chrysler Credit v. Waegele (1973), thus stated this form of injunctive relief varies markedly from attachment or claim and delivery procedures because:

> the use of a temporary restraining order is not confined to matters involving a debtor-creditor relationship, nor for that matter to situations involving property. When * * * a temporary restraining order is used to affect the disposition of property, it does not involve the invasion of privacy attendant on claim and delivery nor does it result in seizure of the property as in attachment or claim and delivery.

While it is possible that a temporary restraining order
may impair the defendant's freedom of use of property, in the ordinary course of events it is not likely
to deprive a person of the necessities of life * * *.

Applications for injunctions are based on assessing the
elements of (a) relative harm, and (b) likelihood of success.
As stated by the court in Sundance Saloon v. City of San
Diego (1989), when

considering the motion for a preliminary injunction,
the trial court must compare the likely harm done the
plaintiff if the preliminary injunction is denied with
the likely harm done the defendant if the injunction
is issued * * * [and] the court must also consider the
likelihood the plaintiff will be successful when the
ultimate issues in the case are tried.

§ 7-6. Receivership

A receiver may be appointed by a court when the defendant is actually or potentially insolvent. Under CCP § 564,
this device is used in the following scenarios:

- involving defrauded sellers who want to keep the
  property sold from being sold or encumbered;

- to safeguard property when there is a substantial
  danger that it will be removed from the state;

- to enforce a judgment; where a corporation is
  insolvent or bankrupt;

- by creditors seeking to set aside transfers that would
  defraud them;

- where mortgaged property is being foreclosed and
  may be destroyed or insufficient to pay the debt.

When is a receivership appropriate, rather than another provisional remedy? Receivers may be used when a creditor has a claim for which attachment is unavailable, or the property is not personal property - for which claim and delivery is the appropriate remedy. Receivers may also sell property, previously seized by attachment. Preliminary injunctions *are* an alternative, and may be used in conjunction with a receivership. Receivership is generally the provisional remedy of last resort, however, due to its very sensitive nature. For example, few owners want an outsider (receiver) to operate their business - even when it is in danger of insolvency or bankruptcy.

There are two alternatives for selecting the receiver. The receiver is usually requested by the plaintiff. Courts also maintain a list of receivers, in the event that a specific individual is not identified in the motion requesting the appointment of a receiver. The court appoints the receiver, who is responsible to the court rather than the plaintiff or any other party.

The receiver's powers to act are established by the appointment order. The receiver's basic obligation is to take protective custody or control of the property, so as to maintain or improve the business or other relevant property interest. The receiver's contracts are normally subject to court ratification. Contracting parties thus deal with a receiver at their peril.

§ 7-7. Execution

Execution is the judgment-related remedy whereby the judgment creditor (JC) enforces a money judgment against the judgment debtor (JD). Money judgments are enforced by the writ of execution. CCP § 699.010. Equity judgments are enforceable by other remedies, including contempt of the court that issued the permanent injunction. Judgments for the sale of real or personal property are enforced by a writ of sale. CCP §716.010. This section of the Nutshell concentrates on execution procedures for enforcing money judgments.

After judgment, the JD has an obligation to satisfy the judgment. If the debtor is unable to do so, or delays satisfaction, the JC may apply for a writ of execution. A separate writ is issued for each county wherein the debtor's property is located.

When granted, this writ is directed to the "levying" officer -typically, the county sheriff. It identifies the parties, amount of the judgment, amount of interest accruing daily, and contains notice of any exemptions claimable by the debtor. The levying officer then executes the writ, by levying upon property described in the writ. This officer sells all non-exempt property and takes custody of non-sellable property such as cash or accounts receivable. The levying officer ultimately returns the writ to the issuing court, with an accounting of action taken and monies received. Costs are payable by the JD.

Exemptions to execution exemptions to execution are contained in CCP §§ 704.010-704.210. They are also listed in a Judicial Council form which must be served on JDs with the notice of execution. They include the following:

- the interest of a partner who is not a JD (when the partnership is not a party);

- debts owed to public entities;

- homesteaded real property; and

- that portion of wages protected from garnishment.

§ 7-8. Supplementary Proceedings

A supplementary proceeding is a post-judgment remedy for satisfying a money judgment. It is supplemental to execution (see Nutshell § 7-7). It is a creditor's substitute for applying for the appointment of a receiver (see Nutshell § 7-6). Such proceedings are initiated by the JC after judgment, and often, after execution procedures are attempted.

This procedure may be used when the writ of execution is returned unsatisfied. Supplementary proceedings may also be invoked in lieu of execution procedures. The JC institutes supplementary proceedings to reach the JD's assets, in order to satisfy the remaining amount of the unpaid judgment. It is appropriate where debtors unjustly refuse to apply their nonexempt property toward satisfaction of judgment. It may also be used as a form of garnishment proceeding to reach third-party debts owed to the JD.

How does the JC conduct supplementary proceedings? The creditor propounds written interrogatories to the debtor, like interrogatories submitted during the pre-trial discovery phase of the suit (see Nutshell § 4-9 on interrogatory practice). The debtor must answer these questions regarding the nature of his or her assets. Failure to adequately respond subjects the debtor to the full range of sanctions available under the provisions of the 1986 Discovery Act. See CCP § 708.020. One limitation is that a debtor's appeal stays the operation of this enforcement remedy.

The JC typically applies for an *ex parte* court order, requiring the JD to appear at the courthouse. The JC then serves a copy of the court order on the JD, no later than ten calendar days before the date set for the examination. Failure to appear subjects the JD to arrest, contempt, and attorney's fees. Third-parties owing money to the JD, and other witnesses, may also be required to appear. The judge or referee conducting the examination may issue a protective order, as justice requires.

At the conclusion of the examination, the court typically orders that property, in control of the JD or third party indebted to the JD, be applied to the satisfaction of the money judgment. The property subject to this disposition must not be exempt from execution (see Nutshell § 7-7 on exemptions). A receiver may be appointed, and the court may thereby expedite execution, if that remedy has not yet been implemented. The court's final order then constitutes a lien on all property subject to the supplementary proceeding.

When a money judgment is satisfied through supplementary proceedings, the JC must file an acknowledgment of satisfaction of judgment. The court then orders entry of this satisfaction into the court's records. That act absolves the obligations of the JD, and releases judgment liens on any other property affected by supplementary proceedings.

§ 7-9. Contempt

Judicial officers possess the inherent power of contempt. Thus, they have the ability to preserve courtroom decorum, and enforce their authority to issue orders prior to judgment.

There are a number of legislatively defined examples of contempt under CCP § 1209(a), including:

- disorderly behavior which disrupts trial or other judicial proceedings;

- falsely pretending to act under authority of a court order;

- disobeying any judgment or order of the court;

- unlawfully detaining a witness;

- disobeying a subpoena; and

- refusing to answer as a witness.

Contempt is summary in nature. When committed in the presence of the court (during proceedings or in chambers), it is summarily resolved by a court order which contains the sentence. When the contempt occurs outside the presence of the court, an affidavit is submitted to the judge, who may then decide the propriety of contempt and the appropriate punishment. CCP § 1211. For example, the court may issue a warrant of arrest. When brought before the court, the contemnor may proceed to obtain an undertaking for the purpose of being discharged from the arrest for contempt.

When an attorney is placed in contempt of court for conduct during trial or any other judicial proceeding, execution is stayed - pending the filing of a writ to review the lawfulness of the contempt order. The attorney subjected to a contempt order has three days within which to file the writ. Otherwise, judicial contempt orders are final and not appealable after judgment.

The legislative penalties for contempt include a fine not exceeding $1,000.00, imprisonment not exceeding five days, or both. CCP § 1218.

There are two general categories of contempt of court: civil and criminal. The distinction is equivocal. If the contempt is "civil" in nature, the court's warrant of commitment specifies what the contemnor must do to relieve the contempt. If the contempt is "criminal" in nature, the contemnor's performance does not necessarily relieve the contempt; or, he can do nothing to purge it.

A jail term may be imposed for either form of contempt. If criminal, the contemnor's jail term is expressly limited by the court's order. If civil, the contemnor may be committed indefinitely. The distinction can thus be quite costly.

The California Court of Appeal made the following distinction, after remand of an appealed contempt case from the federal Supreme Court. In In re Feiock (1989), the California court responded as follows:

> the [federal] Supreme Court opined that a contempt is civil for federal constitutional purposes if the order of contempt ultimately entered allows the contemnor to purge the contempt by performing an act completely within the contemnor's control. * * * If the

contemnor does not have the power to purge the contempt, the proceedings are deemed criminal.

In *Feiock*, the father was ordered to pay child support arrearages during a probationary period. The probation was a penalty for failure to make previously ordered support payments. The contempt order would have been civil, if the probation clearly ended when the last probationary payment was timely made. This contempt was characterized as criminal. The penalty order did not provide for automatic termination of the father's probation, after he was supposed to make the final arrearage payment.

What, then, is the difference between civil and criminal contempt? Unlike civil contempt, criminal contempt triggers federal constitutional Due Process concerns. The contemnor cannot independently purge the contempt, and is thus entitled to notice of the potential sanctions for failure to obey the court's order. Such notice is not required, however, for civil contempt. The federal "ability to purge" approach thus determines whether a contempt is civil or criminal.

California judges tend to apply a more stringent standard for notice. They characterize civil contempt as "quasi-criminal," when there is any possibility of the contemnor's being incarcerated. Thus, California contempt orders require notice of intent to incarcerate, even where the contemnor has the express ability to purge the contempt by his or her independent action ("civil" contempt under the federal standard).

§ 7-10. Costs

The prevailing party is entitled to "costs" as a matter of right. CCP § 1032(b). Costs are recovered from the loosing party, to reimburse the winning party for the recoverable expenses of bringing or defending the action. Costs are separate from the amount of the judgment. Attorney's fees are not included, because they are not costs (unless so authorized, as discussed later in this section).

Do judges have the discretion to award/deny costs? Unlike California judges, federal judges have greater discretion in awarding costs. Rather than *requiring* that costs be paid by the loosing party, FRCP 54(d) provides that "costs shall be allowed as of course to the prevailing party unless the court otherwise directs."

A California judge also has the discretion to deny costs, when the judgment (amount) could have been rendered in an inferior court (or when it is unclear who is actually the prevailing party, as discussed below). A federal judge may also deny costs to - or impose costs on - a prevailing party who recovers less than the $50,000.00 jurisdictional floor for diversity.

Who is the "prevailing party" (PP)? A party who recovers a money judgment is, of course, the PP. A defendant, from whom the plaintiff recovers no relief, is also a PP. When a party obtains something other than monetary relief, the PP is determined by the court. The court has the discretion to deny costs or apportion costs among the parties. A putative father, for example, is considered a PP when the paternity action is dismissed by the court or voluntarily dismissed by the District Attorney.

Costs of a civil lawsuit does not mean *all* costs. It means the legally recoverable costs of suit. The following costs are thus recoverable under CCP § 1033.5:

- costs of filing, motions, and jury fees;

- juror food and lodging, when sequestration is ordered;

- the cost of taking depositions and related travel expenses;

- service of process;

- the expense of attachments and bond premiums, when an undertaking is required;

- lay witness fees;

- fees for court-ordered expert witnesses;

- transcripts ordered by the court;

- court reporter fees;

- models and blowups of exhibits, if helpful to the trier of fact; and

- attorney's fees when authorized by contract or statute (see Nutshell § 7-11).

The above code section on costs is not the exclusive basis for assessing costs. In actions for indemnity or contribution, for example, defense costs may be awarded for proceedings not brought in good faith. CCP § 1038. Costs of initiating supplementary proceedings to enforce a judgment are also recoverable costs. CCP § 685.040.

Costs on *appeal* are recoverable. California Rule of Court 135 (appeal to Superior Court) and Rule 26 (appeal to Supreme Court and District Courts of Appeal) govern the recoverable costs at the appellate stage of a civil suit.

§ 7-11. Attorney's Fees

Attorney's fees are generally borne by each party, regardless of who is the prevailing party. The California Legislature adopted this so-called "American Rule" in 1851. It is the historical barrier against recovering attorney's fees (although permitted in other countries).

The commonlaw basis for the American Rule is the attitude that awarding fees, in addition to costs, would place an unsatisfactory chilling effect on the plaintiff's decision about whether or not to sue (and whether to defend). Many meritorious cases would effectively be denied access to the civil litigation system, due to the considerable "cost" of having to pay the other party's attorney's fees.

There are, however, modern exceptions to this historical limitation in California. Their effect is to characterize attorney's fees as recoverable "costs." The remainder of this section of the Nutshell thus summarizes the key exceptions to the American rule that attorney's fees are not recoverable costs.

CONTRACT Attorney's fees are recoverable in actions on contract, where the parties expressly agree to this result in the event of a dispute. Attorney's fees then become an element of costs obtained by the prevailing party. Civil Code § 1717. Such provisions are typically included in contracts for construction, health care service, real estate services, promissory notes, and leases. *Reasonable* attorney's fees are thus recoverable, pursuant to the terms of the contract. The recoverable fee amount is fixed by the court.

There are limitations, including the following. Actions that are settled or dismissed yield no prevailing party, for the purpose of fee recovery. When tort claims are joined with contract claims, the contractual fees provision allows the prevailing party to claim only those fees attributable to the contract claim.

"998" ATTORNEY'S FEES In 1988, the Legislature passed a special attorney's fees statute. This is a pilot project applicable to all civil actions arising in Riverside and San Bernardino Counties.

Under CCP § 1021.1, attorney's fees may be awarded in cases where the prevailing party has made a Section 998 offer (see Nutshell §5-8). When the offer is refused, and the offering party is the prevailing party at trial, the court has the discretion to include attorney's fees as an element of costs. Such fees are obtainable only for services rendered after the date of the offer.

This pilot project represents a step toward California's adoption of the English system. There, the prevailing party is routinely entitled to attorney's fees. The party who files a non-meritorious suit, or presents such a defense, thus risks the imposition of attorney' fees - contrary to the American Rule. The Legislature has extended the operation of this statute once, and may do so again, due to the litigation backlog in the California court system.

INHERENT EQUITABLE AUTHORITY California caselaw confirms the inherent judicial power to award attorney's fees to the prevailing party. This is another exception to the American Rule against attorney's fees as costs. Three related theories for recovering attorney's fees are thus available, as a result of the California Supreme Court's decision in Serrano v. Priest (1977). In that case, the California Supreme Court effectively established the (1) private attorney general doctrine; (2) common fund doctrine; and, (3) substantial benefit doctrine.

PRIVATE ATTORNEY GENERAL A civil litigant may be considered a private attorney general (PAG), after successfully prosecuting a civil claim which benefits the public. The court has the discretion to award attorney's fees "in any action which has resulted in the enforcement of an important right affecting the public interest" (now codified in CCP §1021.5).

This judicial discretion is legislatively guided by the following principles. The result must confer a significant benefit on the general public or a large class of persons. Pursuit of the action financially burdens the successful litigant. And, the interests of justice indicate that the attorney's fees should not be borne by the prevailing party.

PAG fees are often claimed in cases involving civil rights. The plaintiff alleges a deprivation of rights guaranteed by the federal constitution, triggered by some form of state action. This theory provides the basis for seeking fees (as "costs") under both federal and state law. Sokolow v. County of San Mateo (1989).

COMMON FUND DOCTRINE   The court may also award attorney's fees to the prevailing party who creates a "common fund" for the benefit of a large class of people. This theory is typically advanced in class actions seeking monetary relief. The plaintiff may thus recover fees out of a special fund created by the judgment. Thus, all members of the class -rather than just the plaintiff - pay their fair share of the real cost of the litigation, which includes attorney's fees.

SUBSTANTIAL BENEFIT DOCTRINE   This device is the counterpart to the common fund theory, when there is no fund or monetary relief. The court may exercise its discretion to order fees, if the litigation has conferred a substantial nonpecuniary benefit.

This theory is advanced in cases seeking injunctive or declaratory relief, which confer a benefit on a large class (or a *defendant*). In a successful stockholder's derivative action, for example, a benefit is conferred on all stockholders when the judgment advances the value of the company's stock. The corporation may be required to pay the plaintiff's attorney's fees under this doctrine, because it too has benefitted, as well as its stockholders.

CHAPTER VIII

APPELLATE REVIEW

§ 8-1. Introduction

An appeal permits an appellate court to review the correctness of trial court decisions. There are some policy reasons, however, for limiting such review. The distance in time and location from the trial puts an appellate court in a comparatively poor position to review the factual determinations made by trial court judges and juries. Moreover, broad and unlimited appellate review of factual determinations made by juries is arguably inconsistent with the right to jury trial. Consequently, appellate review of factual determinations is limited (see Nutshell § 8-8).

Nonetheless, the parties to a lawsuit may appeal an adverse decision on an issue of law to a higher tribunal. This chapter of the Nutshell discusses the basic rules which govern this process. At what stage of the proceedings will an appellate court review a trial court decision? What are the time limits imposed on the party seeking review? What is the scope of appellate review?

§ 8-2. Final Judgment Rule

Generally, a party may only appeal final judgments. CCP § 904.1. When a court has determined all of the issues in a case, it enters a final judgment. Consequently, appellate review of trial court orders is typically unavailable when the trial court still intends to address other issues.

The final judgment rule is a basic feature of appellate practice in California. Multiple appeals in a single case would waste judicial time and resources and would be unnecessarily burdensome on the parties. A single appeal, after the trial court has determined all the issues in dispute between the parties, promotes efficiency. The reviewing court can consider all of the claims of error at one time. Moreover, it prevents the interruption of the trial process which would exist if a trial court had to delay its proceedings for appellate review of each decision it made.

Consequently, before attempting to appeal a trial court order, one must normally determine whether the case has reached final judgment. Assume a party appeals from a trial court order, and the case has not yet reached final judgment. The appeal will be dismissed. An appellate court will not even rule on the question of whether the trial court order was correct.

The power of appellate courts to rule on appeals is statutory. An appellate court lacks jurisdiction to hear an appeal unless a statute authorizes it. And the parties cannot confer appellate jurisdiction by their consent or ignorance. Thus, even if none of the parties object to a purported appeal of a nonappealable order, the appellate court should dismiss it on its own motion.

Nonetheless, the appellate courts do sometimes review trial court orders before the case reaches final judgment. The California statutes provide for some express exceptions to the final judgment rule. One such statutory exception is for orders granting a new trial. The grant of a motion for new trial does not suggest that the trial court has resolved all of the issues presented by a case; instead, it means that the trial court will conduct further proceedings. An order granting such a motion, however, is immediately appealable. CCP § 904.1.

Additionally, there are situations where the appellate courts hear appeals from trial court orders before the case reaches final judgment—without express statutory authorization. In essence, the courts find these trial court orders to share sufficient similarities with final judgments to support the exercise of appellate jurisdiction. The sections which follow will summarize these exceptions to the final judgment rule.

§ 8-3. Collateral Order Exception

Matters completely separate from the merits of the litigation may be reviewed before the entire case reaches final judgment. Appellate courts review such orders pursuant to the collateral order exception to the final judgment rule.

California's collateral order exception has three requirements: (1) the decision of the trial court is final; (2) it relates to some collateral issue distinct and severable from the merits of the litigation, and (3) it directs the appellant immediately to pay a sum of money or perform some act. If these requirements are met, then an appellate court can review a trial court order although the case has not yet reached final judgment.

Assume a defendant seeks a trial court order prohibiting a law firm from participating in the case or disclosing certain information to the plaintiff. The defendant alleges that a partner in the firm previously represented him in a related matter. The trial court denied the motion. Would appellate review of the trial court order denying the motion be authorized by the collateral order exception?

The California Supreme Court held that review of such an order was within the exception. Meehan v. Hopps (1955). The court noted that the order was collateral to the merits of the case and that it represented a final determination of the particular issue by the trial court. However, the court did not mention the third requirement. Consequently, subsequent opinions have occasionally found an appeal to be within the collateral order exception without requiring the presence of the third element.

The federal courts recognize the collateral order exception, but never require that the order immediately compel the appellant to pay money or perform some act. Instead, the third requirement imposed by the federal courts is that the matter is completely unreviewable on appeal from a final judgment. As a result, the denial of a motion to disqualify counsel is not within the collateral order exception applied in the federal courts. Firestone Tire & Rubber Co. v. Risjord (1981). In the California courts, because of *Meehan*, denials of such motions are reviewable on appeal before final judgment.

§ 8–4. Sanction Orders

Trial courts sometimes impose monetary sanctions on a party or an attorney for failure to comply with discovery requests or for abuse of the discovery process (see Nutshell § 4-16). The orders imposing such sanctions appear to meet all three requirements of the California version of the collateral order exception. However, the California courts find that the exception is inapplicable to such orders made under the authority of to the discovery statutes. Slemaker v. Wooley (1989). These orders are so numerous that such recognition might undermine the purpose of the final judgment rule. On the other hand, the courts deem sanction orders made pursuant to other provisions, such as CCP §128.5 (see Nutshell §§ 3-10 and 4-17), to be within the exception.

In 1989 the California Legislature amended CCP § 904.1 to provide that an appeal may be taken "[f]rom a superior court judgment directing payment of monetary sanctions by a party or an attorney for a party only if the amount exceeds seven hundred fifty dollars." The amendments clearly changed the rules regarding the appealability of sanction orders, but there is some controversy regarding the nature of those changes.

Some appellate courts find that the Legislature intended to create a "bright line - $750 - above which immediate appellate review is authorized and to eliminate the distinction between types of sanction orders. Greene v. Amante (1992). Under this view, if a discovery statute sanction or a CCP § 128.5 sanction is greater than $750, it is immediately appealable. If either type of sanction is less than that amount, it is not appealable before final judgment.

Other appellate courts emphasize that the legislative intent behind the 1989 amendments was to restrict the category of appealable orders. They also contend that the Legislature was aware of the distinction the courts had made between appealable collateral orders and nonappealable discovery sanctions. These courts conclude that if the Legislature had intended to make discovery sanctions appealable, it would have done so clearly. Consequently, they find orders imposing monetary sanctions under the authority of the discovery statutes - regardless of the amount - to be appealable only after final judgment. See, e.g., Ghanooni v. Super Shuttle of Los Angeles (1992). Other sanction orders are immediately appealable, if and only if, they exceed $750.

§ 8-5. Multiple Claims and Parties Exception

If there are several parties and claims in a lawsuit, generally there is not an appealable final judgment until all the claims involving all the parties have been resolved. Even where there is only one plaintiff and one defendant, the trial court cannot enter a final judgment on one count when others remain unresolved.

The California courts, nonetheless, recognize several exceptions to this limitation on appellate jurisdiction. First, if the trial court has resolved all of the issues to be determined as to one party, those determinations can be appealed.

Assume that there are two plaintiffs, P1 and P2. P1 is asserting only one claim against the defendant, but P2 is asserting two. If P1's claim is dismissed before the court resolves all the other issues in the case, P1 can appeal the dismissal. An appellate court can rule on the merits of P1's appeal, although P2 claims are still pending in the trial court.

Another exception exists when an appeal has been improperly filed before final judgment, but the trial court has subsequently resolved all of the remaining issues. To prevent unnecessary delay, the appellate court amends the judgment on appeal. It then construes the notice of appeal as relating to the amended judgment.

Suppose a plaintiff filed a complaint containing two counts. Before trial, the trial court dismissed the first count and purported to enter a judgment reflecting that decision. Plaintiff then filed a notice of appeal. Later, after a trial, the court entered another purported judgment in favor of the plaintiff on the second count. Neither purported judgment is an appealable final judgment. The appellate court could dismiss the appeal. It would then instruct the trial court to amend the latter purported judgment to include its dismissal of the first count. Yet, all the issues have been resolved; there is no reason for it to delay its review. Therefore, the appellate court will likely amend the judgment itself and treat the notice of appeal as being from the amended judgment.

The California courts have also recognized an exception in cases where the trial court has severed a count or counts from a complaint for separate trial. Thus, if the trial court dismisses the severed count and it is separate and distinct from the others remaining to be tried, the judgment of dismissal is appealable. The courts consider a severed count to be separate and distinct, if it arises from a different transaction or occurrence.

In the federal system, FRCP 54(b) contains specific provisions for cases involving multiple claims or multiple parties. If the district court has reached a final decision on one or more of the claims, but not all of them, it may take steps which will permit an immediate appeal of that decision. It may make "an express determination that there is no just reason for delay" and "an express direction for the entry of judgment." If the district court properly exercises its discretion in taking these steps, the decision may be the subject of an immediate appeal. Otherwise, any appeal must await final judgment.

§ 8-6. Extraordinary Writs

In unusual circumstances, the California appellate courts may review lower court decisions pursuant to extraordinary writs - although the particular decision is not appealable. The most important extraordinary writs are writs of mandamus or mandate and writs of prohibition. Writs of prohibition are used to prevent judicial acts in excess of jurisdiction. CCP §1102. Writs of mandate are used to compel performance of ministerial duties. CCP § 1085.

Both writs require a showing that the remedy at law is inadequate. CCP §§ 1086 and 1103. Consequently, the reviewing court must determine that its consideration of the issues presented cannot await an appeal after final judgment.

Assume that a defendant seeks a writ of prohibition on the grounds that though the trial court lacks subject matter jurisdiction over the case, it has denied a motion to dismiss. Participation in an unjustified trial and a subsequent appeal from an adverse judgment is not an adequate remedy. The writ, consequently, is available to determine whether the trial court properly denied the motion to dismiss for lack of jurisdiction.

Appellate courts may grant extraordinary writs because the issues raised are of such public importance that expedited appellate review is necessary. For example, in Brown v. Superior Court (1971), the Secretary of State sought the imposition of penalties because the defendants failed to comply with disclosure requirements required by election campaign statutes. The trial court sustained a demurrer on the ground that the statutes were unconstitutional. The California Supreme Court decided to bypass the normal appellate procedures and review the trial court decision. It based its decision on the public importance of campaign disclosure laws and the controversy surrounding them.

In some unusual cases California appellate courts have treated appeals from nonfinal orders as petitions for extraordinary writs. In such cases the appellate courts may decide to review the case pursuant to the extraordinary writ. However, to justify such treatment the circumstances must be compelling enough to establish the propriety of the extraordinary writ in the first instance.

On the other hand, California law makes writs of mandate routinely available in some situations. For example, when a trial court denies a defendant's motion to quash service on the grounds of lack of personal jurisdiction, the defendant not only has a right to seek a writ of mandate to obtain appellate review - she must. See CCP § 418.10. If she does not, she will be deemed to have waived her jurisdictional objection and cannot raise it on a subsequent appeal from a final judgment.

§ 8-7. Timeliness of Appeals

To appeal a trial court order or judgment, a party must file a notice of appeal in the trial court. Generally, notice of appeal must be filed within sixty days of the earlier of the following two dates: the mailing of a notice of entry of judgment or appealable order by the clerk of the court, or the service of such a notice by any party. California Rule of Court (CRC) 2. Both the party who submitted the judgment or order and the clerk of the court must mail such notices to all the parties to the action. CCP § 664.5 In the unlikely event that such notice is not provided, then the notice of appeal must be filed within 180 days of the entry of the order or judgment.

The time to file a notice of appeal is extended in some situations. For example, if a valid new trial motion is served, filed, and denied, the time for filing a notice of appeal is extended until thirty days after entry of the denial. CRC 3. Notwithstanding any such extension, a party wishing to appeal must file the notice within 180 days of the entry of judgment—the outside limit for filing notices of appeal.

The appellate courts strictly enforce these time limits. Hollister Convalescent Hospital, Inc. v. Rico (1975). A reviewing court may, for good cause, relieve a party from a failure to comply with the rules governing appeals - *except the failure to file a timely notice of appeal.* CRC 45(e). In Estate of Hanley (1943), the California Supreme Court explained this limitation as follows:

> In strictly adhering to the statutory time for filing a notice of appeal, the courts are not arbitrarily penalizing procedural missteps. Relief may be given for

excusable delay in complying with many provisions in the statutes and rules on appeal, such as those governing the time within which the record and briefs must be prepared and filed. These procedural time provisions, however, become effective *after* the appeal is taken. The first step, taking of the appeal, is not a procedural one; it vests jurisdiction in the appellate court and terminates the jurisdiction of the lower court.

Because the issue is jurisdictional, the appellate courts do not have the power to grant relief from the late filing of a notice of appeal.

In the federal courts, a party wishing to appeal generally must file a notice of appeal within thirty days of the entry of the order or judgment. FRAP 4(a)(1). As in the California courts, the time may be extended by the timely filing of certain motions after trial, such as a motion for new trial. Thus, if a new trial motion is denied, the thirty day period for the filing of the notice of appeal runs from the entry of the order denying the motion. FRAP 4(a)(4).

Unlike California's courts, federal courts have the discretion in certain situations to extend the time for filing a notice of appeal. The party seeking the extension must do so within 30 days after the expiration of the normal period for filing the notice. FRAP 4(a)(5). If the motion is filed after the running of the normal period, the appellant must establish "excusable neglect" for the failure to file within the period.

Assume that a party relied upon the actions or representations of the court or its officers in good faith. As a result, she did not file a timely notice of appeal. A federal court may find the party's conduct to be excusable neglect and grant an extension. See Redfield v. Continental Cas. Corp. (1987).

On the other hand, if the appellant seeks an extension while he still has a right to file the notice, then the lesser showing required by the "good cause" standard suffices. Any extension granted cannot exceed thirty days beyond the period in which the notice could have been filed as a matter of right or ten days after the extension order, whichever is later.

§ 8-8. Substantial Evidence Rule

Appellate review of factual determinations made in a trial court is limited. A California appellate court can overturn a decision on a factual matter made by a trial court or a jury only if that decision is not supported by substantial evidence. If such a decision is supported by substantial evidence, it must stand - even if the appellate court disagrees.

Substantial evidence is relevant evidence which a reasonable person would accept as adequate to support the determination. A scintilla of evidence will not suffice. Moreover, it must be the type of evidence which, if true, would have probative force on the issue. In deciding whether substantial evidence supports the decision below, the appellate court must accept all the evidence favorable to it as true, and the unfavorable evidence should be disregarded.

§ 8-9. Harmless Error Rule

An appellate court cannot set aside a judgment or order a new trial because of trial court errors which are harmless or not prejudicial. Cal.Const.Art.VI §13. A trial court error is prejudicial if, after examining the entire case, it seems probable that a result more favorable to the appellant would have been reached, if the error had not occurred. The reviewing court will consider the total circumstances of the particular case. Often the strength of the evidence in support of the judgment will be a key factor. The risk is greater that an error influenced the result in a case in which the evidence was close than one in which it was extremely one-sided.

Appellate courts must often determine whether an error is prejudicial when they conclude that the trial court gave an erroneous instruction to the jury. They must decide whether it seems likely that the jury's verdict was based upon the instruction. In deciding that question the court will consider several factors. They include: (1) the degree of the conflict in the evidence on the relevant issues; (2) whether the respondent compounded the error by making arguments to the jury based upon the instruction, and (3) whether other instructions may have had the effect of remedying the error.

CHAPTER IX

PRIOR ADJUDICATION

§ 9-1. Introduction

A prior case may affect a current one in various ways. For example, a court will not allow the relitigation of claims which have already been adjudicated. Also, a party to the current suit may be bound by the resolution of an issue in previous litigation. Finally, courts will often look to, and follow, the decisions of other courts which have decided the same legal issues. This chapter of the Nutshell will address the ways in which current litigation may be affected by previous decisions.

"Claim" and "cause of action" are used interchangeably in the Nutshell. The term "res judicata" will be used to refer to preclusion doctrine generally. Thus, res judicata includes both "claim preclusion" and "issue preclusion." Claim preclusion refers to situations where a party is precluded from litigating a claim because it was litigated in a previous suit. Issue preclusion refers to situations where a party has litigated an issue in a previous action and is bound by its resolution in it. Nonetheless, some courts and writers use res judicata to mean only claim preclusion and use the term "collateral estoppel" for issue preclusion.

§ 9-2. Stare Decisis

When the California Supreme Court decides a question of California law, its decision must be followed by all the lower courts in the state. The doctrine of stare decisis mandates that once an issue has been resolved by a higher court, the lower courts must abide by that resolution-even if they disagree. Thus, if the California Court of Appeal has adjudicated a particular question, superior courts throughout the state have to apply its decision. However, if two or more panels of the Court of Appeal have reached different conclusions, then the lower courts may choose from the various resolutions of the matter.

Another aspect of stare decisis reduces the likelihood of such conflicts. Prior decisions by the same court or other courts on the same level are generally followed. They are followed though the current members of the court might resolve the issue differently in the absence of the previous decision. Thus, stare decisis promotes the predictability and stability of the legal system. The public can rely on earlier legal determinations, with the understanding that future courts are likely to apply them. Rapid and unexpected changes in the law are therefore unlikely.

Nonetheless, stare decisis does not mean that courts can never reconsider or overrule previous decisions. Instead, it is a flexible doctrine which recognizes that in certain circumstances it will be necessary for courts to reexamine their previous determinations.

A California court may consider several factors in deciding whether to overrule or modify a ruling made in an earlier case. One factor which the California Supreme Court may consider is whether the courts of other states have adopted its approach or rejected it. The more uniform its rejection by such courts the more likely the court will reconsider the issue. Scholarly criticism is likely to be treated similarly. If the reaction of legal scholars has been overwhelmingly negative, it argues in favor of the court examining the issue again. Another factor is whether the previous decision has had adverse social consequences. Such consequences, especially those which were unforseen at the time of the initial decision, may induce a court to revisit a previous decision. Additionally, a California court may consider whether lower courts have had analytical difficulties in interpreting and implementing the previous decision. Such factors are weighed carefully by a court in deciding whether to reconsider a previous decision. However, a decision to revisit a previous holding does not necessarily mean that it will be overruled.

§ 9-3. Res Judicata Generally

Res judicata is based upon the policy that all litigation must end. If the disputes submitted to litigation were open to endless reevaluation followed by different resolutions, then litigation would not be an efficient or effective way to resolve controversies. Thus, res judicata encourages reliance on and respect for the judicial system by preventing inconsistent decisions.

Res judicata also seeks to prevent the waste of judicial and private resources a scheme of endless litigation would entail. The conservation of limited judicial resources serves the public benefit, and the parties are relieved of the cost, burden, and harassment of multiple lawsuits.

§ 9-4. Claim Preclusion

A claim cannot be relitigated in a subsequent suit once it has been presented for adjudication, and a valid and final judgment on the merits has been rendered. If the claim is asserted in a later judicial proceeding and the defendant raises the defense of claim preclusion, the court should dismiss it. Claim preclusion does not affect the court's jurisdiction, however. Thus, if the defendant does not raise the defense, then the court will adjudicate the claim despite the prior proceedings.

A judgment is valid for preclusion purposes if the court which rendered it had personal jurisdiction over the defendant and subject matter jurisdiction over the case. Consequently, although it may be clear that a previous decision was incorrect, the judgment is not for that reason void or invalid.

Under California law, suits are not final for claim preclusion purposes until all appeals have been determined, or the time to appeal has expired. On the other hand, federal law provides that federal court judgments are final for claim preclusion purposes when the trial court enters a final judgment. Thus, although an appeal is pending, the federal courts consider the judgment final. If the trial court decision is reversed on appeal, then it loses its preclusive effect. Additionally, a court may set aside any judgment based upon the reversed judgment and make provisions for restitution of any benefits received pursuant to it.

Claim preclusion prevents relitigation of not only the issues which were actually litigated in the first suit, but also those which should have been raised. Even if the plaintiff makes additional or different factual allegations in a second action on the same claim, claim preclusion will prevent relitigation. Similarly, the plaintiff cannot avoid claim preclusion by arguing different legal theories in the second suit. The additional or different factual allegations or legal theories should have been raised in the first lawsuit. The plaintiff's failure to do so will not lead to a second opportunity to litigate the claim.

§ 9-5. Scope of Claim

Courts have used several different definitions for claim or cause of action. The California courts use the *primary rights test* to determine the scope of a cause of action. Under this test a cause of action is not simply a set of facts making up a transaction or occurrence, but the unlawful violation of a right which those facts show. If the second suit seeks to vindicate the same primary right as the first, then it asserts the same cause of action. Slater v. Blackwood (1975). Conversely, if the second action seeks to vindicate a different primary right than the first, then it asserts a different cause of action-even though it arises from the same transaction or occurrence.

The most significant factor in determining the primary right or rights involved in a particular case is the harm suffered. Consequently, incurring two or more kinds of harm in a single transaction or occurrence may give rise to two or more causes of action.

Assume that D's car collided with P's car. P suffered both personal injuries and damage to his car. P could sue D for his personal injuries and then bring a second suit for damage to his car. The second suit would not be subject to dismissal pursuant to the doctrine of claim preclusion. It presents a different cause of action than the first. In the first suit P sought to vindicate his right to be free from injury to his person. P asserts a separate and distinct right to be free from injury to his property in the second suit. Because it seeks to vindicate a different primary right, a California court would not dismiss it under the doctrine of claim preclusion.

Federal courts, however, use the *same transaction or occurrence test* to define claim or cause of action. Pursuant to that test a subsequent suit asserts the same claim as a previous one, if both arise out of the same transaction or occurrence. Thus, the claim is the group of facts which make up the transaction or occurrence.

Reconsider the hypothetical collision mentioned above. In the federal courts P could not bring a first suit for his personal injuries and a second suit for damage to his car because of claim preclusion. The second suit presents the same claim because it arises out of the same transaction or occurrence, i.e., the same collision as the first.

Courts consider several factors in deciding whether the facts alleged in the second suit are part of the same transaction or occurrence as those presented in the first. These factors include the following: (1) the relationship between the facts in time, space, origin, or motivation; (2) whether the two groups of facts would have made a convenient trial unit, and (3) whether treating them as a unit is consistent with the parties' expectations or busi-

ness understanding.   See Restatement (Second) Judgments, § 24 (1982).

Despite the apparent differences between the two approaches, the California courts sometimes apply the primary
right analysis in a manner which closely resembles the same
transaction or occurrence test. One plaintiff challenged an
administrative determination that she be dismissed from her
position as a teacher in her first suit. She contended that the
evidence did not support the finding that she was incompetent. The court, nevertheless, upheld plaintiff's dismissal.
In a subsequent suit plaintiff alleged breach of her employment contract, intentional and negligent infliction of emotional distress, and wrongful discharge for exercising her
first amendment rights of free speech and association. The
California court held that both suits were based upon an
alleged invasion of her contractual right to employment.
Takahashi v. Board of Education of Livingston, Union
School District (1988). There was only a single harm
suffered. All of her alleged causes of action in the second
action arose either in conjunction with or as a result of the
alleged invasion of this single primary right. She had sought
to vindicate the alleged violation of this right in the first
action. Such a broad analysis of the primary right involved
leads to the same result as the same transaction or occurrence
test.

On the other hand, the court could have concluded
that the right to be free from emotional distress was
separate and distinct from the plaintiff's contractual
right.   The court could have found that the federal
constitutional rights relied upon by the plaintiff in the
second suit were separate and independent of the state

law contract right she sought to vindicate in the first. See Agarwal v. Johnson (1979). Because there is no precise test to decide what constitutes a single primary right, sometimes the test is easy to manipulate.

§ 9-6. Issue Preclusion Generally

Issue preclusion (collateral estoppel) prevents a party who litigated an issue which was essential to a previous judgment from relitigating that issue. The doctrine is based on the notion that once a party has a fair opportunity to litigate an issue, she should be bound by its resolution. She should not be allowed to litigate the matter again. Thus, even if the second suit presents a different claim, its outcome may be determined by an earlier action.

Refer to the hypothetical car accident discussed above involving P and D. P suffered both personal injuries and damage to his car. The California courts would recognize two claims arising out of the accident. P could bring an action for personal injuries and then later bring a subsequent suit for property damage. However, if the jury in the first action decided that D was not negligent and entered a judgment for him for that reason, D could rely on that finding in the second suit. P would be prevented from relitigating the question of D's negligence. In other words, P would be estopped from trying to persuade the finder of fact in the second action that D had been negligent.

However, certain requirements have to be met before issue preclusion will operate. First, the issue must have been actually litigated in the previous action. Second, the issue must have been essential to the judgment rendered in that action. The next two sections of the Nutshell will address these requirements.

§ 9-7. Actual Litigation Requirement

Issue preclusion will only operate if the issue was actually litigated in the previous lawsuit. Unlike claim preclusion, it is not enough that the matter could have been raised in the earlier suit. For example, the California courts will not allow issue preclusion to be used in a civil case against someone who entered a guilty plea in an earlier criminal proceeding. Teitelbaum Furs, Inc. v. Dominion Ins. Co., Ltd. (1962). In such a situation, there has not been a presentation of evidence and arguments on the issue of the defendant's guilt and to allow issue preclusion would deprive the party who entered the guilty plea of the chance to make such a presentation for the first time. However, if the defendant had pleaded innocent and had been found guilty after a trial, issue preclusion would be available. He would not be permitted to litigate the issue again.

Because of the actual litigation requirement, the courts of most states and the federal courts do not give default judgments issue preclusive effect. However, the California courts have in effect created an exception to the requirement. They give issue preclusive effect to the essential elements of the cause of action which were set forth in the pleadings in cases where a default judgment has been rendered.

§ 9-8. Essential to the Judgment

Issue preclusion also requires that issues which a party is being estopped from relitigating were essential to the judgment in the previous case. The courts will not prevent a party from relitigating unnecessary or unimportant findings in an earlier case.

Refer to the hypothetical car accident between P and D discussed above. Assume that in the first action P sought to recover for his property damage. D argued that P was guilty of contributory negligence. Contributory negligence was a complete bar to the D's liability under the applicable law. The jury returned a verdict that both P and D had been negligent. Consequently, a judgment was entered for D. If P brings a subsequent action seeking to recover for his personal injuries, D will not be estopped from relitigating the question of his negligence. Although the jury in the first suit concluded that D was negligent, that finding was not essential to the judgment. An essential finding was that P was guilty of contributory negligence because the judgment for D was based on it.

§ 9-9. Parties

Issue preclusion prevents relitigation. Thus, the doctrine can only be *asserted against* parties to the previous action or those in privity with such parties. In this sense a person is in privity with a party when the relationship between the two is such that it is fair to bind her to the resolution of the issues in the previous case. For example, if the party in the previous case was a fiduciary representing the interests of a particular indivual, that indivual is bound by the previous decision. The counstitutional right to due process of law imposes an important requirement on a court's ability to subject someone to either issue preclusion or claim preclusion. The person against whom preclusion is asserted must have either been a party in the previous suit or had her interests adequately represented by one who was a party. If a party in the previous suit was neither a fiduciary nor a class action representative, the courts will not find that she adequately represented the interests of any other person. Thus, issue preclusion is usually available only against parties to the previous action.

Similarly, the traditional rule was that only those who were parties to the prior litigation *could assert* issue preclusion. This requirement is called "mutuality of estoppel." A party who wished to rely on estoppel had to have been in a situation where she faced the risk of having the issue resolved against her in the prior litigation.

Most American jurisdictions no longer impose the mutuality requirement. The leading case abandoning the requirement was decided by the California Supreme Court.

In a probate proceeding Bernhard and the other beneficiaries under the decedent's will contended that the executor of the estate, Cook, had to account for funds which he had transferred from the decedent's bank account before her death. After a hearing on the charge, the probate court found that the decedent had made a gift of the funds in the account to Cook. Subsequently, Bernhard sued the bank at which the account had been kept. She claimed that the bank was liable for the money which had been in the account because the decedent had not authorized its withdrawal. The defendant bank had not been a party in the earlier probate proceeding, and thus, there was no mutuality of estoppel. Nonetheless, the court held that the defendant bank could assert issue preclusion against Bernhard. It concluded that there was no reason she should be permitted to litigate the issue again simply because she changed opponents. Bernhard v. Bank of America (1942). Thus, the defensive use of issue preclusion is available against a complaining party who has litigated the same issue earlier against a different adversary.

However, the converse situation, the offensive use of issue preclusion without mutuality, has produced some uncertainty. This problem arises when the defendant has litigated the issue and lost, and a plaintiff tries to use issue preclusion to establish some portion of his claim. The United States Supreme Court rejected a wholesale ban on the offensive use of issue preclusion without mutuality in Parklane Hosiery Co. v. Shore (1979). It held that the offensive use of the doctrine should be allowed unless the plaintiff seeking to assert it could have easily joined the first suit or the use of the doctrine in the circumstances of the case would be unfair to the defendant. The Court indicated that the use of issue preclusion would be unfair in the following situations: (1) if the defendant had little incentive to litigate the issue in the first action; (2) the judgment relied upon was inconsistent with one or more previous judgments in favor of the defendant, or (3) if the second action afforded the defendant procedural opportunities which were not available in the first and could readily lead to a different result. The California courts are following this approach. See Imen v. Glassford (1988).

§ 9-10. Intersystem Preclusion

Article IV section 1 of the United States Constitution and its implementing statute, 28 U.S.C. § 1738, require the states to give full faith and credit to the judicial proceedings of other states. These provisions reflect concerns about comity; consequently, the courts have interpreted them to allow the states to determine the preclusive scope of their own courts' judgments. A California court must give a sister state judgment the same claim preclusive and issue preclusive effect that it would have in the court which rendered it. See Marrese v. American Academy of Orthopaedic Surgeons (1985). Similarly, a California judgment has to be given preclusive effect in accordance with the rules described in this chapter in any state court in which it is presented.

Assume that in the first action the plaintiff failed to amend the complaint after the sustaining of a demurrer. The State X court consequently entered a judgment for the defendant. Plaintiff then files a second suit in a California court based upon the same cause of action. In the California suit the plaintiff includes allegations in the complaint which were not contained in the complaint filed in the first action. In this way the plaintiff hopes to defeat a demurrer based upon the same grounds as the one asserted in the first suit. Under California law such a second action containing different or additional allegations is not barred by claim preclusion. Nonetheless, the California court would have to dismiss the second suit pursuant to that doctrine - if the law of State X provides for preclusion in such cases.

The full faith and credit statute generally requires federal courts to give claim and issue preclusive effect to state court judgments whenever the courts of the state which rendered them would do so. Congress has the power to make exceptions to this rule, but in the absence of the exercise of that power the federal courts must accord preclusive effect to state court judgments. See Allen v. McCurry (1980).

Some have contended that all cases within the exclusive jurisdiction of the federal courts are exceptions to the full faith and credit statute. However, the federal courts have rejected this argument. Instead, they have found the issue to be whether in providing for exclusive federal jurisdiction Congress intended to deny preclusive effect to state court actions in the particular context. And they have generally answered the question negatively.

State courts must give federal court judgments the same claim and issue preclusive effect that they would be given in a federal court. Thus, a California court in deciding the preclusive effect to be given a federal court judgment must look to federal law.

INDEX

References are to pages

References are to pages

References are to pages

References are to pages

References are to pages

References are to pages

References are to pages

References are to pages

References are to pages

References are to pages

References are to pages

References are to pages

References are to pages

References are to pages

References are to pages

References are to pages

References are to pages

References are to pages

References are to pages

†